LIFE
CHANGING
Sex

Susanne Wendel

authorHOUSE

AuthorHouse™
1663 Liberty Drive
Bloomington, IN 47403
www.authorhouse.com
Phone: 833-262-8899

Published by AuthorHouse 01/18/2024

ISBN: 979-8-8230-1585-1 (sc)
ISBN: 979-8-8230-1584-4 (hc)
ISBN: 979-8-8230-1583-7 (e)

Library of Congress Control Number: 2023919289

Print information available on the last page.

Any people depicted in stock imagery provided by Getty Images are models, and such images are being used for illustrative purposes only.
Certain stock imagery © Getty Images.

This book is aimed at mature, healthy adults and sexually mature youths. Unfortunately, in the area of sexuality, not only the highest peak experiences open up, but also the deepest human abysses. Those are explicitly not the point here. This book is about getting to know and exploring one's own sexuality deeper and trying out things that one has not dared to do before. The author specifically distances herself from all practices that do not take place between adult people and in mutual agreement because these are the basic conditions for a fulfilling sexuality.

This book is printed on acid-free paper.

CONTENTS

Contents

PREFACE

Man passes by a little open garden of paradise
indifferently and becomes sad when it is closed.

— Gottfried Keller

My beloved readers, you may be asking yourselves how someone could come up with the idea of writing a book with her own sexual experiences —and a woman, at that. It's very simple: I think it's time to see sex for what it is. Sex is quite different from what we think. It can be vulgar, it can be surprising and it can be an enormous amount of fun. So much fun that we "do it" again and again and sometimes put everything else in our lives at risk for it. The topic of sexuality is surrounded by many myths, fairy tales, mindfucks, and even garbage, and I think it finally needs a book that is honest, that doesn't come around the corner with clever advice but describes sex as it often is, which is quite complicated. On one hand, sex is the most natural thing in the world, a deeply human, basic need. Evolution has arranged it over millions of years so that we enjoy it. And from a purely biological point of view, sex is intended for people from puberty onward. Even if it's difficult for us to imagine at times, we are here in this world today because our parents successfully had sex! On the other hand, we humans have imposed so many taboos on sex over thousands of years through culture and religion and have tried to regulate it so much that hardly any adult person can deal with it in an unbiased way. What I also illuminate in this book is that sex is by no means only for reproduction and short-term fun.

I am originally a health expert and I promise you: Sex makes you healthy physically, mentally, and spiritually! Pleasurable sex is enormously important for our development and evolution, just as healthy food and drinks provide the right nutrients, sleep relaxes us, and spiritual pleasures inspire us and make us happy. There are now tons of studies and research that prove that sex stimulates the immune system and prevents diseases and can even cure them in some cases. This is especially true for the "fashionable diseases" of heart attack, depression, and burnout; it plays a significant role! According to experts, people in the professional group that most often suffers from burnout—even before managers—are, according to all accounts, Catholic priests. Unfortunately, no studies exist yet on the effects of suppressed sexual desires. It's about time! Sigmund Freud, Carl Gustav Jung, Wilhelm Reich, and other psychologists and physicians researched these topics at the beginning of the twentieth century. Not only does sex have a positive influence on our physical health, fulfilled sex lives make us mentally healthy. I would even go so far as to say that the "right" sex brings us closer to enlightenment faster and easier than the individually appropriate yoga, meditation, or fasting method. Yoga is socially accepted as a way of achieving relaxation and spirituality. But sadomasochism? Or group sex? Can you imagine that these can also heal people mentally? I can—because I have experienced it. The fact that I can say today that I am really satisfied with my life has a lot to do with the fact that I have explored my own sexuality. I dared to let fantasies and dreams become reality. I would like to pass on this experience, however it may manifest itself in someone else. This is only possible if you let go of prejudices and become curious.

It's different than what is commonly thought. And above all, it is very, very individual. That's why this book features some other people who have found their way to fulfilling sexuality in very different ways, including laughing, hitting, using toys, making porn movies, and engaging in "silent sex," where they don't do anything at all.

Discover your favorite sex. Find out what sexual identity you have and what is your Life Changing Sex. And you will experience a new quality of health and joy of life that you did not know before.

With this in mind, I wish you a lot of fun with *Life Changing Sex*!

ACKNOWLEDGMENTS

Many people have inspired me over the past years (among them many men, of course). To all of them I would like to express my deep gratitude.

And there are some few people, who have actually transformed me into the person who I am today. They have caused me to shift my personality. Before, I was the typical single after divorce—hard working, no relationship, and no-family-kind-of person. I went from a mainstream ecotrophologist, giving seminars about nutrition in pharmacies and writing books about diets——to finding my true passion and living it *all!*

Happy family. Happy sexlife. Happy relationship, Happy and successful professional life—I became a provocative speaker in front of big audiences with the topic of *sex* and a well-known and appreciated author on the topic of *sex.*

I could not have dreamed about it because back then I had *no clue* about my true essence and my true desires for my personal and my professional life.

It took a quantum leap and complete transformation, which started with my participation in a ten-day leadership training, "The Arts of a Woman," in Maui, Hawaii, with Sonja Becker and her team at Wailea GmbH & Co KG. I continued in Capetown in 2008 with a four-week high-performance leadership training, "Adventure Team".

Sonja Becker is a pioneer of the twenty-first century for thirty years with a clear vision of the essence of people, giving them the courage to live *their* dreams in life. Sonja leads people to become self-actualized and free human beings with character. Without

Sonja, this book would not exist because I would not be the person who I am today.

I had to get rid of many fears, prejudices, and illusions. And for this, I needed people who believed in me more than anyone can do by oneself. Over the last seventeen years, Sonja Becker has encouraged me to follow my own curiosity. Through Sonja and her team, leadership and business skills with power and tailwind came into my life! At this point, I would also like to thank Irene Xander, who is a great role model for me in terms of freedom, leadership, and business. People who go their individual ways experience true freedom and true love.

With this book I hope to inspire you to go for *your* true self and find out who *you are* and live accordingly!

Finally, I would like to thank my partner, best friend, bodyguard and husband, Frank-Thomas Heidrich, who has my back in all things and who can allow his wife to write such personal books.

INTRODUCTION TO THE ENGLISH-LANGUAGE EDITION

Life Changing Sex: The original title in German is *Gesundgevoegelt*, which cannot be correctly translated into English. It means something like "fucked to health." Well, sex makes you healthy, especially very good sex—everybody knows that. This book was and is very successful in German-speaking countries and has already inspired thousands of people to live a more open, freer sex life. Ten years after the first publication in Germany, I translated the book into English. I have written five more books about sexuality and relationships and have had two children since then. I also studied for five years and completed a master's degree in applied sexology, in addition to my other professional activities as a speaker and sex coach. Life Changing Sex makes people not only healthy but also happy and powerful. I live a very powerful relationship with my husband, and we develop together and challenge each other every day. The best sex of your life is no coincidence.

For many years I asked myself how I could bring my book from small Germany into the big world, and I hesitated because I was sure that there are already so many sex experts everywhere and so many books about the topic, so who needs mine? But what I became aware of through many trips in recent years is that hardly any other country has so many people who are as sexually free as those in central Europe. In hardly any other country is sexuality in all its facets lived out so openly and celebrated so much. Especially in the last few years, in the German-speaking world there has been grown a gigantic stronghold of hedonism.

This book is about true sexual freedom. I was one of the pioneers, particularly for women, to finally dare to strive for my own sexual self-realization and to let others share their real experiences. I am very curious about how you will like it and look forward to your feedback.

Chapter 1

OVERSEXED AND UNDERFUCKED

Everything we suppress puts pressure on us. And pressure makes us sick. Accept who you really are, and it will be easy.

Without the animal in us, we are castrated angels.

—Herman Hesse

P ROBABLY, EVERYONE HAS SOME SPECIAL inclination in bed. Why should we all tick the same way in this area of all things? Everyone is a unique individual. Everyone likes different things to eat and has different hobbies, dreams, and talents. So when it comes to sex, are we all supposed to be the same? Very unlikely. What unites us all is the desire for sex. This is a deep, basic need like eating, drinking, and sleeping. But just as one person likes sushi, another likes roast pork with dumplings, and a third likes deep-fried grasshoppers, there are huge differences in how we like sex. Maybe we have a special "favorite sex," maybe we prefer variety, or maybe we enjoy both. Some people are rather conservative about it, and others like to try new things. The beauty of it is that everyone is allowed to be who they are. But the question is, what are you like?

1

The dilemma is that we are so shaped by our cultures, religions, and upbringings—and in case of doubt, also by our partners—that we don't even know what we want, what turns us on, or what makes us happy. At most, we notice only by chance when we particularly like something.

I suspect that most people actually have no idea what their sexual needs are because they never ask questions about it. Or they secretly know it very well but do not dare to tell anyone for the rest of their lives, let alone try it out. At most, they secretly search for it on the internet. Parental imprints and societal moral codes are extremely strong and can plunge people into terrible conflicts when they discover that they are deviating from the norm. Thank God, a lot has already changed in this regard in recent years and decades. Homosexuals are now socially and politically recognized and well organized. No one has to be ashamed or alone anymore—superficially, at least. I don't want to know how many families deal with drama when parents learn their children are gay or lesbian. Probably far more people have homosexual tendencies and still find it very difficult to come out. It may be that their desires are so repressed that they don't even notice it themselves, except perhaps in the fact that they don't really enjoy sex. Maybe they dream about it at night. No one can look into another person's head. And what about sadomasochists? Having fun with submission and pain is far from socially acceptable. What about people who are into fetishes and toys, who love anal sex, or who have experienced sexual abuse and are not healed? Those who don't shuffle through life completely apathetic will sooner or later come to a point where they feel the animals in them, want to express their innermost needs, and want to experience what gnaws at their souls. If morals, fear, distorted values, and false consideration stand in the way, pressure arises.

This pressure makes one sick. It does not find the right outlet. It is directed against the family, colleagues, employees, and in the worst case children. Ultimately, it is directed against oneself. The person becomes mentally and physically ill. There are no studies on this, and so far, nobody has examined how pressure from repressed sexuality affects people. I think it is devastating. Sigmund

Freud, the founder of psychoanalysis, addressed this issue over one hundred years ago, and Alfred Kinsey, in his large-scale sex report on America in the 1960s, found that many more people than assumed had homosexual or other "deviant" sexual preferences. Deviant from what? Sexuality is one of the strongest drives that people have. Otherwise, we would not have been walking around and reproducing on this planet for many millions of years. We cannot pretend that this is not important. What the various media outlets want us to believe about sex is often very far from reality, especially from the reality in our bedrooms. And deep down, we know that too.

We are oversexed and underfucked.

This sentence brings it right to the point, as does the subtitle I just read on a german book: *Why We Talk More and More about Sex and Still Don't Have Any.* Why is it so? Perhaps because we are overwhelmed and unsettled by the variety of possibilities. It's as if we were standing in front of a huge buffet with lots of things we don't even know—some tempting, others repulsive—and ultimately, we have no idea what it all tastes like. Or perhaps, in our fast-paced times, we no longer dare to love wholeheartedly and truly engage with another person. "Is Our Life Too Exhausting for Sex?" was the headline of a major German women's magazine recently. The article was about how typical young adults today—regardless of whether they have children or not—have so much to do every day that there's simply no energy left for sex in the evening. Various experts were consulted and questioned, and they concluded that modern people are overwhelmed by their lives and have less desire than before. Is it really so? I don't know if it was less strenuous for our ancestors to work in the fields all day or to take care of the household of a large family. But satisfying and liberating sex is never too strenuous because you have more energy afterward.

But what really is satisfying sex? What does it mean for you? This is where the expedition begins. I would argue that most people have never or very rarely experienced the best sex of their lives outside of their heads.

Now, I admit that sex is something that requires at least one other person for optimal results. And that is often a challenge. How do I find the right person who likes exactly what I like? Alternatively, how can I teach my partner, who is already by my side, to have sex the way I like it? Is that possible at all?

When it comes to the best sex of your life, when was the last time you had it? Have you even had it before?

If I had not searched determinedly and found the people with whom I can talk openly about everything that goes around in my head, I certainly would not have told anyone or tried it. You can only find the right sex and conversation partners in a suitable environment.

In Japan, you will not likely find the best curry sausage. But if you do, then the provider is certainly German. Likewise, seek contact with people who are sexually free. An acquaintance of mine was married to a man for years, gave birth to several children, and raised them. Only in her early forties did she realize, more or less by chance, that she enjoyed sex with a woman much more than anything she had experienced before. She once told me about the moment when her blindness fell from her eyes like scales: "Oh, that's how it is! So this is fulfilling sex; this is what it feels like." I don't know the details, but I suspect it must have been similar to someone experiencing an orgasm for the first time after only hearing about it up to that point. Should we leave something so important to chance?

I would not call myself a "sexpert." I am not a sex therapist, a psychologist, or a dominatrix but a normal woman—admittedly, a curious woman and certainly a little more determined than average. I did make my deepest desires and fantasies come alive. It is possible to live everything that is in us. It doesn't happen overnight, and it takes a whole lot of courage. But it is worth it. For me, it was and is the most fulfilling journey of exploration I have undertaken so far. Some say, "You can't have everything," as if to say, "When it comes to love, sex, and partnership, you always have to compromise." Not true! If you make too many compromises, you kill the best in yourself.

Do you want a mediocre life or a brilliant life? That is a decision everyone has to make for themselves. Life Changing Sex doesn't come with compromises. You have to be willing to pay the price for your freedom—that's clear. But the reward is many times higher.

This book is not a guide to a better sex life, because there are no instructions for living a horny life correctly. You can only find out for yourself and explore what it is for others personally. In this book I describe my very own story, my experiences, and everything I have experienced and learned about men, women, and sexuality. Many things I experienced exactly as I have described them; other things—for example, the names of some of the people involved—I have changed. I did a lot of research and consulted experts. Furthermore, I interviewed quite "normal" people. I would like to encourage women and men to stand by their wishes and to dare to share them with their partners. It is worth it! Maybe you're thinking now, *What? Should I open a new construction site and take care of that too? Isn't what I'm already doing enough? I have so much work to do. I go to the gym, I regularly go on a diet and do autogenic training, and now I'm starting to work on sex. Besides, that's not so important.*

Please, it is your decision. Nobody has to do anything. But to work on *this* brings much more to your life than everything else you work on. There is no stronger force than the sexual one. And activating it and guiding it in the right direction will bring you more power in all other areas of your life. Every man in his midforties who falls in love with a young woman and suddenly feels unexpected strength again knows this. Every woman knows this when she meets a fantastic lover and can finally let herself fall into his arms. So let's make something out of it! Let's start researching and begin to find out who we really are. This journey goes through ups and downs, over beautiful peaks, and into deep, hidden, dark caves. There is much to discover, some amazing, some uncomfortable, but ultimately all relieving! Find out if you prefer sushi or roast pork—or both or neither. It will make "shopping" easier in the future. And you'll discover a new dimension of health and joy of living.

Do you know the man with the saw? The one who struggles all day to cut down a tree and works on the tree for hours with a blunt saw and only makes progress millimeter by millimeter?

Someone comes along and asks him if he wouldn't like to sharpen his saw first, then it would be easier. "No, I don't have time for that!" grumbles the annoyed man and continues sawing. How about taking a little time to sharpen your saw? Good news: Sex is the fastest way to sharpen a saw! (modified. after Stephen Covey, *The 7 Habits of Highly Effective People*)

Chapter 2

SEX BETWEEN THE EARS

About society, the human brain, and sexuality today. And about the freedom to be who you are.

If everything were satisfactorily
arranged in the world ...
we would have learned in seventh grade sex
education that there are such and such.
It would be self-evident to us that sexual
preferences turn out as differently as musical ones,
and we wouldn't be ashamed of
some more than others.

— Kathrin Passig and Ira Strübel
("The Choice of Agony")

GRÜNWALD, JULY 2012. OUTSIDE, ONE of the many violent storms that simply won't let you relax on these hot summer days is raging. Perfect for writing a sex book. The world is ending around me, and I finally know how I want to start this book. The idea of writing it has been haunting me for years. Now I'm finally ready to do it. Because only now do I know what I actually want to say. In a way, I feel like I've found myself. It took long enough. And somewhere, it's also clear that, at the same time, I'm right back at the very beginning. It's always like that in life.

Yes, I love loud techno music, and yes, I'm into giving up control during sex. I give talks to hundreds of people for fees that other people have to work two months for. I'm an entrepreneur, coach, and multiple book author. I'm almost forty, I love group sex and "sadomaso" parties, and I'm pregnant. I have a wonderful partner who is also my business partner, manager, and bodyguard, and he does everything he can to make me happy and successful. And it all fits together wonderfully. Why not? Today, we are in a time when everything is possible—theoretically, at least. All of us can live exactly how we want and as it is good for us. But when I look around, I see that most people have not yet realized this. They lead lives that are shaped by the thoughts and laws of their parents, their families, and society, which has not yet understood that things change faster than any system can react to them. People adapt to somethings that often no longer exist. They do it this way, they do it that way, they think about it that way, simply out of habit and because our brains are structured in such a way that they copy behaviors that were once successfully rewarded again and again, even if the rewards no longer exist. "You have to eat everything on your plate" is such a classic. Despite extra-large portions and excess weight, their main concern is that nothing is left over. I've studied a lot of biology, psychology, and modern brain research, and I'm also a coach. I'm simply interested in how people work or function and why. I simply want to know how they can change because most of them are not really happy in their lives. To understand how change is possible, you must understand how the human brain works. I highly recommend to everyone regarding this topic is reading Professor Gerald Hüther, a neurobiologist at the University of Göttingen. In his book *Operating Instructions for a Human Brain*, he summarizes the human dilemma wonderfully:

> We do not possess a brain capable of learning throughout our lives so that we can settle comfortably in life with it.... Of course, we have the freedom to

stop at any time where it pleases us, and henceforth
to use only those circuits which have been formed
in our brain up to that time. But since these circuits
are all the more efficiently pathfinded, the more
frequently we use them repeatedly in the same way,
it could easily become the last free decision we have
made in our lives. (p. 119 in german book)

Humans are incredibly flexible and adaptable, and at the same
time, they are not at all. Modern neurobiologists like Hüther confirm
quite clearly that the brain is plastic, and our neurons can forge new
paths until death. But this requires something very special: a strong
state of arousal, either joy or fear that is so intense that it knocks
our socks off. Only then are neural pathways switched on—when
something really touches us deeply. Boredom, habit, and routine
lead directly to a neurological dead end from which we cannot get
out at some point.

It takes a stimulus that is stronger than habit, an experience
that literally throws us off course in the truest sense of the word.
That's how we can change with emotions. To stabilize this new state,
routine is necessary but only until something new occurs again. The
way I have found to give my life more fulfillment is through sex.
There may be others, but I believe this one is very efficient, if not
the most efficient, because it is one of the very few paths lined with
constant excitement that simultaneously brings to light everything
that makes a person unadulterated and honest. Those who discover
their own desire are clearly at an advantage. But this is exactly where
the dilemma begins.

We live in a society where anything is theoretically possible
sexually and we have anytime-anywhere access to sex, but deep
down, we are shaped in such a way that most of it seems dirty
and somehow wrong. So we prefer to leave it alone, instead maybe
getting inspiration from movies, pictures, and stories, but in the
end, everything is in our heads and stays there. I would even go so
far as to say that many people don't even get the idea that in lived,
fulfilling sexuality lies the key to important changes in their own

lives. How and from where? You don't learn something like that in school or at the university.

Societal systems react infinitely more slowly than individuals, and many rules, once installed in a society, last for generations. Systems want to control people and to scare them. When people are free and self-sufficient, they no longer need systems. But how can you become free if you are so influenced by the system? Where do we really stand today on the subject of sex? The entire society is still influenced by a two-thousand-year-old religion that wants to make us believe that almost everything that is fun is sin. Even in our parents' generation, or at least our grandparents', people thought they got pregnant from kissing. Sex before marriage was taboo. Cheating was a crime. Even today, this is still stuck in people's minds: anything that deviates from the normal bedroom sex of a monogamous couple is at best suspicious and at worst anything from perverted to mentally ill. Many variants of sexuality that are quite common today are still listed in the worldwide catalog of diseases published by the World Health Organization (WHO). And this classification is based on a system that is almost 130 years old.

The most obvious of all diseases is not listed anywhere, although almost all adults suffer from it: chronic loss of vitality. Its cause is years of adjustment to a life that prevents development, fun, and growth; that suppresses talents, desires, and preferences; and that tries to create well-behaved conformist do-gooders who function. But at some point they think, *That can't be all yet!* They are people who put on one mask after another for years in order to be liked everywhere, who don't even know what they really desire anymore behind all the niceness, and for whom sex is about as exciting as showering. Everyone has good and bad sides, light and dark. The dark one often shows itself unadulterated in sexuality, as Freud already described. It is a force that comes from the deepest depths, a drive that can destroy everything and create new life at the same time. It is a huge gain to look at and explore this side. Without it, our lives are half as exciting—and half as honest.

He who hides his dark side has boring sex. You'll have the best sex of your life when you stop holding anything back, stop trying to look good, and stop pretending to be anyone else. Achieving this state, however, takes a lot of courage and curiosity. And it can take time—sometimes half a lifetime, sometimes just a single night.

For many years, my dark sexual side was one thing above all: embarrassing! I dreamed of being tied up, of being helpless, of being controlled. I don't know where something like that comes from. As a young woman, I often wondered if I would have to see a psychiatrist one day. Today I know that a lot of women—if not most of them—have such fantasies. But none of them talk about it! Even at the thought of telling anyone what I wanted during sex, I used to blush bright red. And I usually never blush. But finally, I met people who feel the same way I do, who have similar thoughts and desires, and found myself in an environment where the abnormal was suddenly normal. We spent evenings chatting amusingly about handcuffs and bondage techniques, just as others chat about new knitting patterns. It was there that I first realized how much we humans are shaped by our environment, by our fellow human beings and by society. With these new people, it´s suddenly easy I can let go and open up. It is just like a plant that needs a lot of light but has been standing in a dark room: it suddenly blossoms when you put it by the window.

What do the five most important people in your immediate environment think about sex? The answer to this question shows you where you stand. Your environment has a huge influence. Find out about my life changing experiences in the following chapters and awaken you own curiosity.

Chapter 3

LIFE CHANGING SEX

For most people, sex is about as exciting as taking a shower. What kind of sex does it take to change your life?

If he wanted me, even if it was only for one night, I was ready to give up everything. My whole fucking future. Everything.

— Alice Harford (played by Nicole Kidman) in *Eyes Wide Shut*

WHILE RESEARCHING THIS BOOK, I stumbled across an interesting article and the following quote from sexual sociologist professor Werner Habermehl: "60 percent of people have never had a particularly impressive sexual experience. For them, sex is about as exciting as taking a shower." He says this in the context of a study on Life Changing Sex. Allegedly, more and more people are looking for it. The desire of men and women to finally experience Life Changing Sex is increasing, triggered by the huge supply of sex in the media, where sex is always portrayed as mindblowing.

This desire of many people perhaps explains the great success of Internet affair exchanges, which deliberately bring sex-hungry people in contact with one another. So much for "partners for life." Here it's all about erotic encounters; most of the listed members are married or in committed relationships and are looking for nothing more and nothing less than the ultimate kick through cheating. Likely, they believe that there is no way they can experience that in their partnerships.

What Is the Sex That Changes Lives?

Most of the time, Life Changing Sex happens unplanned, often with a stranger or in an unknown place. Afterward, nothing is the same anymore. People leave partners and families, their familiar surroundings, and their lives because they have experienced through sex that there is more and now suddenly feel new vitality and a deep longing that they did not know before. Normally we are stuck in our habits, but when something like this happens to us—when we are literally torn out of our usual paths by such a strong impulse—new doors open. Everyone knows stories of people who suddenly turned their whole lives around after falling in love again. The question is, is it possible to experience Life Changing Sex without letting it collapse all of one's life?

The affair exchanges are certainly an attempt in this direction, but they won't work for everyone. The fact is that, in order for something new to come into life, something old has to die, something that you previously thought would always stay the same. This doesn't always have to be the relationship. Sometimes it's something that you previously considered to be the truth.

In my life, however, this meant that I had to give up my marriage. Because with the partner I had at that time, it would not have been possible to explore what my soul wanted to explore.

There are certain key experiences through which I realize that something new is about to happen. Most days are somehow similar. And then there are the days after which nothing is the same anymore, such as when someone dies, when a child is born, when we separate, when we move, when we get to meet a person who upsets us, or when we have sex that is so different from everything before.

Winter 2004. The first event that threw me off track was an encounter at a party with a man with whom I fell madly in love. Until that evening, I was more or less happily married, my life was more or less pleasantly calm, and everything to that point had been plannable. This is not to say that I hadn't always been spirited, fun-loving, a little crazy, and fond of flirting with men, but I was faithful and content in my relationship, and that would have gone on forever. The sex was good and regular, although mostly a compromise for me because my husband could do little with my very specific wishes in the direction of being tied up. He liked "field-forest-and-meadow sex," as he called it, and what I imagined did not turn him on. If he did it for my sake, it was still a compromise, for both of us. Nevertheless, we had a strong connection. My marriage had just survived a major crisis; my husband was abroad; we talked on the phone several times a day; and one day I went to this party. At that time, I had been professionally self-employed for some years, knew very well what I wanted, and was talking business with the party guests when I happened to sit next to this cute business consultant who told me very privately about his failed engagement and later asked me to dance. Other than talking, dancing, and a little flirting, nothing happened. I still don't know exactly what happened to me that night, but it felt like a fuse blew—an important one. I couldn't sleep that night, and that was just the first of many. I also couldn't eat for days and couldn't think clearly for weeks, except about this man. Scientists claim that the state of being in love is similar to that of an obsessive-compulsive neurotic who has to wash his or her hands all the time because of a lack of serotonin in the brain. Looking back, I have to say that's true!

Much later, I realized that all this didn't have so much to do with this guy but with myself and with the fact that my life was going to blow up in my face one day. And it became quite clear to me quickly that my husband and I would separate. There were many other reasons, and suddenly we had the right trigger.

Spring 2005. It was the first time I thought I should do something really crazy. I was still thinking about this management consultant, even though he didn't want anything from me, and daydreaming about what it would be like to invite him for a weekend in an expensive hotel. Something like that. The thought came while hiking. I was alone in the Black Forest for two weeks, wanting to clear my head after it was foreseeable that my twelve-year relationship and eight-year marriage would soon be over. I had booked myself into a small hotel to think about what I actually still wanted in life. On a Tuesday, after breakfast with fresh grain porridge, fruit, and organic milk, I knew: My life had become boring, well-behaved, and predictable, and that did not correspond to my nature at all! All of a sudden, it was clear to me. This wasn't me, and it should end immediately. *Do something crazy, Susanne, something with which you surprise yourself!* As clear as the thought was on that sunny spring morning, I soon forgot it just as quickly as it had come. I had no idea what crazy thing I should do. Over the previous few years, I had become so accustomed to my relaxed, planned life and my partner that I had no idea what else was inside me. Really no idea at all.

But I had planted the seed, and it began to germinate. Not much later, it happened almost on its own. Being single was not my thing. And so, just three weeks after finally separating from my husband, I was already registered on several dating sites. I don't do things by halves. One of the first curious people was a young master baker from Hannover. He seemed so incredibly nice, funny, and polite at the same time, and I thought he was just great. What we shared was a passion for techno music. He wrote about his favorite techno disco in Hannover, and it was clear to me that I had to go there! So I bought a train ticket, booked a room at the ETAP Hotel and went to Hannover. What was the worst that could happen? I had a bunk bed at ETAP, and I would survive one night. As I said, I do not do things haphazardly. We met at the station, and with a look, a sniff, and a hug, it was clear that the evening would be cool. How cool? First of all, we would get to know each other, eat ice cream, check each other out, and make those first little touches. Maybe all that doesn't sound so spectacular, but for me, it was a revelation.

I could never have imagined feeling as free and good as I did that evening. For the first time in at least ten years, I was back in a disco with a man I didn't even know! Suddenly it was very real, and it was fantastic. *That* was crazy. And in a strange way, it was natural for me. What strange ideas we all have in our heads of what is good for us and what we want. We don't even know what the world has to offer, and we forget what once made us happy. We look through frosted glass with a tiny little hole. For me, I would consider a man for a partner only if he was a university graduate. He had to be just as intellectual and brainy as I was. And above all, everything always had to be planned, preferably sex as well. And now I was on a date with a master baker? So spontaneous! Well, he was in quite good condition and had strong arms. After all, he kneaded a lot of dough every day.

That night healed a piece of my soul that I didn't even know was sick. I felt a deep liveliness that had been lost to me.

And I knew: That's *me*. We danced until five in the morning. Back at the hotel, we had sex the rest of the night until breakfast, I think four times in a row. Life Changing Sex. It was so *different*— different movements, different touches, a different feeling. And bunk bed, my ass. We didn't need that at all. I had no guilty conscience, no fear, no stupid feeling, no morals, nothing. It was natural. That night, I felt who I really am for the first time in a long time; it was the feeling of someone who is much more at home in the body than in the head. I would not have thought that sex with a stranger could be so exciting. I had only ever slept with one man, and then I married him—the same man for twelve years. And three weeks later, I was with a new one on the very first evening. Is that allowed?

Well, if I think about it correctly, I had already had many encounters and relationships with men before my marriage. They were also almost always spontaneous and also got very physical quickly. We did everything at that time except sexual intercourse in the narrower sense. Where does sex actually begin and where does it end? Maybe I hadn't discovered anything new that night in Hannover but only rediscovered something old. Maybe that suited me much better than living with the same man for twelve years. Such passionate, spontaneous, crazy actions and encounters give me an incredible amount of energy. I'm like that—I can go all out right away. I don't need a long warm-up phase. I can tell immediately if someone fits. What should I wait for then? I had previously heard instructions like, "You have to get to know the men first; you have to hold back at the beginning and don't reveal so much about yourself!" But men are not made for me. What a relief to realize that!

That night in May 2005 was the beginning of a new phase in my life. I was in for it; I wanted to break out of myself. I wanted more liveliness again, more *me*. For that, a part of my old life, my habitual thinking, had to die, which is totally natural. Torment and thus pressure arise because we cannot let go.

What is your truth about relationships and sex? Which mask has to fall with you? What may die with you, and what wants to arise new? What makes you feel alive and awake and gives you power? What is your Life Changing Sex?

I made a start with the master baker. That was my first Life Changing Sex, and I knew there was no going back. I didn't want to go back at all. We were together for three months, meeting even more often, in Hannover, at a disco in Berlin, and in Munich. I felt free, although at the same time I was sad about the end of my marriage. However, to turn my favorite secret fantasy into reality took a few more experiences, men, disappointments, and overcoming a whole bunch of prejudices and fears. To become truly free takes years.

Chapter 4

LOOKING THROUGH
THE KEYHOLE

**Sex clubs are playgrounds for adults. People
in erotic clubs care more about health,
hygiene, and respect than most other people.
And they have more fun during sex too!**

Most of all, when you get older, you
regret the sins you didn't commit.

— William Somerset Maugham

VISITING A SWINGERS CLUB IS something that many people think
about doing at some point in their lives, but swinging still has
a stigma of being disreputable, immoral, and dirty. Due to diffuse
fears and prejudices, even many curious people never set foot in
such an establishment. Too bad. Because fun, respect, and hygiene
are the top priorities. And the scene is growing. It's hard to find
concrete figures. However, one thing is clear: the trend toward
"special" sex is unstoppable. Some statistics claim that there are
now about two thousand swingers clubs in Germany, and erotic fun
portals like JOYclub have millions of users. Beyond that, you can
even find hotel and wellness facilities, cruises, and motorcycle trips

for swingers. By the way, the concept of partner swapping is not so new. The first media reports on the subject of "wife swapping" appeared as early as 1957 in an American men's magazine. At that time, such exchanges were more likely to occur privately or at special parties. Getting ahold of the relevant information and addresses was certainly much more difficult in the past than it is today. And yet the hurdle is still very high for most people today. I can only say, Have the courage to go in! You can only know definitely whether you like it or not after you experience it. In my own experience, the surprise factor is extremely high in everything related to sex.

I can decide very quickly when I want something and am curious about something, sometimes so quickly that I wonder at myself. In the afternoon, I may still be planning to prepare my nutrition lecture for the next day, and in the evening, I may find myself on a mattress with a complete stranger I didn't even know until that afternoon. I am curious by nature about everything that has to do with sex, including erotic clubs. I'm sure not everyone is. And most of the people I know only talk about it and then don't do it. They probably never dare enter these mysterious walls anytime in their whole lives.

Many prefer to stick to their uninformed opinions about it, telling themselves that only ugly people go to those places anyway, they are unhygienic, people get diseases there, and so on. But the reality is genuine, honest, and actually quite different! Many people simply do not know what awaits them there or, above all, what is expected of them.

The first time I went to a swingers club, I had many questions: What do I wear? What shoes? What do I have to take with me? Do I have to shave beforehand? Does everyone do it with everyone there, and what if I don't want to do it with everyone?

I was lucky thought. I went there with someone who knew his way around and explained everything to me beforehand. The only risk for me was that I did not know *him*. My first time in a swingers club was also my first date with a man I had seen for the first time in front of the entrance. One could think that was already a pretty high risk. On the other hand, I thought the risk of someone doing something to me that I didn't want was probably much lower in a club than anywhere else.

The day was a Friday in January 2006. Friday the thirteenth was *the* Life-Changing-Day for me, and I was there with a man I would like to call Mr. Darkmind. He was ultimately the one who opened the door for me to explore my sexual depths. Before that, I was comparatively well behaved. I got to know him through one of the many Internet dating portals. His profile, Darkmind, appealed to me very much because he wrote something about "devotion," "being able to drop," and a "strong hand." I had no idea what exactly he meant by that, but it turned me on. The humorous and pleasant correspondence that followed aroused my curiosity about this man. The whole thing took place at a time when I was giving a lot of lectures and seminars and was extremely busy on the road. I will never forget that Friday afternoon when I was at home briefly between two seminars, repacking and doing laundry. That afternoon we spoke on the phone for the first time. Like me, Mr. Darkmind came from North Rhine-Westphalia and spoke pleasant High German. You never know which dialect is hidden behind an internet profile. I personally do not find some dialects very erotic, and I live in Bavaria, after all. Well, he didn't, in any case, speak any dialect, and he sounded nice and funny and was sympathetic to me right away. When he asked me if I would like to accompany him to an erotic club in Munich in the evening, I spontaneously answered, "Yes, of course!" The lecture on healthy weight loss that I was to prepare for the next day went far away in one fell swoop. I would have plenty of time for it on the train the next morning, I figured. I've always been curious about what a swingers club looks like from the inside and what goes on there. And Mr. Darkmind just sounded so incredibly seductive and, at the same time, confidence-inspiring on the phone. If so, then I would go with him. Today.

There were also a few things to sort out: What on earth should I wear? For women, this was actually simple. I listened, spellbound, to his words through the phone as he told me to preferably wear beautiful lingerie and high heels. Apart from the fact that I did not have a single pair of high heels in my closet at that time, I was confident. My lingerie could be seen. And the idea of sitting half-naked at a bar didn't bother me either.

A friend of mine has not dared to go to a club even to this day because she says that exact thing would not work for her, sitting in lingerie somewhere where other people are watching. Actually, it's the same as wearing a bikini at the beach bar, I say.

Mr. Darkmind explained to me that outfits were a much bigger problem for men. Men's underwear is just usually not very sexy. Shoes are even more tricky. Sneakers? Sandals? Possibly with socks? For the sake of simplicity, many would fall back on slippers, but that would tend to reduce their success with the women that evening. He himself always wore a pair of chic loafers without socks, a nice pair of underpants, and a black T-shirt.

Suddenly, in the middle of the conversation, I became aware that I was becoming immersed in a world in which the clocks tick differently. At that moment, I was suddenly wide awake and, at the same time, everything seemed surreal. And this incredibly intense experience of the moment lasted the whole evening. This must be that moment that meditation gurus talk about when you are completely in the here and now and experience the present. Right at that moment, after about an hour and a half of talking on the phone, I thought for the first time that I must be pretty crazy already! I was there on the phone with a complete stranger and talking about the swingers club's dress code. Mr. Darkmind and I made a date for 8:00 p.m. When I hung up the phone, I still had two hours. And then I was really nervous! Shower, do my hair, put on makeup, and change clothes. Awesome. That's exciting!

I cleared out everything that I could find and needed from my closet and decided on my black negligee, including a thong and a pair of halfway passable, half-height black pumps. For today, this outfit would have to do. At half past seven, I got into the car and turned up the techno music as loud as possible. Pure adrenaline shot through my veins. Excitement. *Excitement*. I'm sure I've never been so nervous in my life. And I know this is one of those evenings that I would think back on for the rest of my life. It was a moment when time stood still and I wouldn't know afterward whether it had lasted a minute or an eternity.

When parking, my hands were shaking so badly that I could hardly steer, but I finally made it to the parking space at 8:00 p.m. *I'm on time,* I thought. *I'm on time. Right on time!* So I was there, and so was he! He looked just as friendly as he sounded on the phone. I was lucky; it sometimes works. With him, I could dare to go in there. His humor was also there. We started laughing together right away, and I began to relax.

We went to the entrance area, payed the admission fee, and then we went to the communal changing room. There were closets for the clothes and a blue towel for everyone. *Like at the swimming pool*, I reassured myself.

The first thing you do in a swingers club is to order something to drink at the bar. The entrance fee includes unlimited drinks. Anyway, where do you put a wallet when you're half-naked? We sat down at the bar and drank. The voice in my head was getting really loud again: *Susanne, you're totally crazy!*

The second thing you do in a swingers club is eat. That is also included in the price, and it tastes very good. This club had a huge buffet with everything anyone could wish for. However, I could hardly eat anything that night because of all the excitement, but I did have a few shrimp, a roll of ham with asparagus, and a piece of roast beef.

The people were nice, open-minded, very friendly, and pleasant. I did not expect that at all. *You must be joking,* you may be thinking. *Only pot-bellied, back-haired Neanderthals go there, and most are not even very good-looking!* There were many couples, some of them older people, and no one was even slightly pushy. We could sit down anywhere in the cozy seating areas and eat in peace or watch the others, make out a little, and let ourselves be carried away by this very special flair.

After the second glass of white wine, Mr. Darkmind accompanied me upstairs to the floor with the mattresses. *Aha,* I thought, *so this is where it gets down to business.* I must say that, up to this point, I had never watched other people have sex live. This is probably the case for most people. Sex is generally done in pairs, maybe even in the dark, and definitely without an audience. When seeing it live, it suddenly became much more real, very different than in the cinema or on TV. The people there were real, and if I wanted to, I could join in right away. At that moment, when I saw the first couple on the wide mattress in a kind of cage, it flooded through me: a tingling sensation of a very special kind that I have experienced many times since. How exciting!

On the first floor were many rooms, full of nooks and crannies, all differently furnished and decorated. There's something for every preference. You'll find jungle flair, Oriental touches, and cages that allow people to watch but restrict others from joining in. Everywhere on the mattresses were small baskets with condoms, tissues, wipes packs, and small trash cans. Everything was taken care of there; it was clean and pleasant. Not much was going on at the time; some guests roamed around and looked where there was already something to see. The attractive couple behind bars already had a lot of spectators, and I watched fascinated as she lolled under his kisses. I had really never seen anything like this before, at least not a meter in front of me. We moved on to the next room. There, a woman gave herself to a whole horde of men, who dutifully stood in line and waited their turn. *Gang-banging is not my thing*, I realized immediately. *How could a woman like such a thing?* I found it exciting that no one was bothered by the spectators. Those who wanted to went after their desires, and I got the feeling that they even liked to be watched. Everyone enjoyed one another's fun, and most were having a lot of it. The exceptions were men who came alone; they had to see where they were welcome. Couples or single women walking down the aisles could expect a whole bunch of men to follow them. Bizarre, but true. So do we, Mr. Darkmind and me, as we walk through the rooms. Behind us were six men, all wearing shorts and slippers and holding towels. *No wonder my companion doesn't come here alone*, I thought to myself, and I couldn't help but smile.

Drunk from these first impressions, I went up one floor with Mr. Darkmind, where the large dessert buffet was set up today.

Tiramisu, crème brûlée, and chocolate mousse in large bowls appeal to the only remaining senses that are not yet awakened. We took a small bowl with us and ordered cocktails.

I was wide awake, sucking up everything like a dried-up desert flower. It was awesome! What a fascinating world, so different and yet somehow familiar. We sat down on a couch, talked, laughed, and got into conversation with a very nice couple. They were from Stuttgart and were spending a wellness weekend in Munich. Aha—the kids were with Grandma. I was so fascinated by this conversation, the sensual atmosphere, and the people, and so completely immersed in this bizarre situation, that my brain felt like it was shutting down. The next thing I consciously remember is that I was lying on a mattress between Mr. Darkmind and the woman from Stuttgart. My companion whispered quietly in my ear that he never has sex in the club on the first date. He was a pro; good to know. What felt like an eternity later—but was probably only ten minutes—I wondered what time it was. Almost forgotten but coming through again was my common sense! After all, I had to leave the house at 5:30 the next morning to take the train to Münster, where I would tell 250 pharmacists at the university how to lose weight most effectively—oh dear, I hadn't prepared the lecture yet! I hadn't packed my suitcase either. And my clothes were lying in front of the closet since I had cleared out everything randomly. At that moment, I had the feeling of floating above my body. One part of me was lying on the mattress and melting under the touch of several people I don't even know, while another part of me briefly switched on its brain. The brain took over, observed the human tangle, and asked me, *Susanne, what are you doing here?*

The answer to this question came to me sometime the next day on the train between Dortmund and Hamm: *I'm alive!* I had discovered something that is definitely my thing, something that totally turns me on, something that, even in my wildest dreams, I would never have thought would fascinate me so much. And I also realized that this was just the beginning. I had entered a new world, like Alice in Wonderland.

This is not to suggest that everyone will or must like such

experiences. But if you never try it, you can't know. Definitely not. I certainly didn't know before. Maybe a lot of people are afraid of "getting something" in a club like that. I didn't think that at all, but I'm not usually anxious, either. But for all those who have this thought in their heads, let me say: swingers are very concerned about hygiene and health and usually deal with the subject much more responsibly than other people. Anyone who falls in love "out there" and gets into bed with a stranger after the third date—or possibly on the very first evening—also doesn't know who the other person is and what they have. People often don't know themselves! The most important thing in the club is that you pay attention to hygiene, be careful with any exchange of bodily fluids with strangers, and do nothing you do not want.

A clear rule among swingers is "A *no* is a *no*!" And as a rule, everyone adheres to it. Anyone who wants to make contact with someone and join in touches them on the arm, and the person touched is free to accept or reject the request. How far one wants to go is up to each person. Politeness on both sides is the top priority. There are showers, towels, and condoms everywhere, and it is normal for everyone to use them. When you have gotten rid of the last of your clothes, it is best to sit or lie down with your bare bottom on a towel. For those who are afraid of AIDS, this disease is much less common in European countries than hepatitis, for example. The biggest health risk in sex clubs is catching a fungus or bacterial infection, which can be completely prevented with condoms. You should also consider kissing or having oral contact with a stranger, as viruses and bacteria can be transmitted in this way. If necessary, you can limit yourself to activities that do not involve the exchange of bodily fluids, such as massaging and caressing. Then you are on the completely safe side.

In good clubs, there are bulk packs of massage oils or body lotions; you can have a lot of fun with them. By the way, for oral sex with a strange woman, there are so-called licking cloths instead of condoms for those who want to play it safe. On the other hand, I think you should not worry too much; otherwise, the fun will fall by the wayside. By the way, many people deliberately do not have sexual intercourse in the narrower sense with strangers in the club, and that is not expected. What is required, however, is a high level of hygiene. Showering beforehand and, if necessary, in between is a must, as are clean clothes, towels, and good personal hygiene. Intimate shaving is not necessarily expected but is desired by many. Of course, it is up to each individual to decide whether to allow strangers to penetrate these zones at all. By the way, most guests at clubs are couples, and you can be sure that health, hygiene, and respect are just as important to everyone else as they are to you. I personally believe that people who regularly go to sex clubs are healthier overall than others, at least those who take their chances there simply because they are freer, more relaxed about sexuality, and able to live out many of their fantasies. Also, they are aware of the risks and are therefore more careful with their bodies.

They are probably less likely to have depression and heart attacks because they keep tapping into a source of energy and happiness that is hidden from most people. And they are happier because they live who they are and can relieve pressure very effectively. That would be an interesting study, but unfortunately, no one has commissioned it yet.

How high is the risk when actually compared to the gain of expressing ourselves sexually and freeing up our main channel of happiness? I have spent some of the most brilliant, most beautiful, and happiest evenings and nights of my life in this and other clubs. More happiness hormones were released than my immune system could ever use. What fascinates me so much is that every evening is completely different. You never know who's going to be there and what you and others are going to be in the mood for and what's going to develop. Whoever gets involved can only win.

Chapter 5

BEING HORNY IS ALLOWED!

If you take off the masks of morality and fear, together with your clothes, new worlds open up to you. If people were more satisfied in the area of sexuality, there would be fewer wars in the world!

Sin is the invention of unhappy people who
could not bear to see others do well.

— Lady Maria in *24/7: The Passion of Life*

EXPERIENCING THE WORLD OF EROTICISM is always a real event for me, even today, whether it's a club, party, fair, or private meeting. Each time, I feel as if I am diving into a new world, into an enchanted fairy-tale landscape where clocks and people tick differently. It's different every time; you can't have any idea beforehand what will happen. Every club is different, and the people are different every time. Maybe that's the special attraction. You can't plan an evening like that. I love diving into these other worlds. Does that make me abnormal? Do I have to be ashamed because I like this kind of thing? In the end, I just tried it out because I wanted it and curiosity was greater than anything else. For me, going to clubs is quite normal, just like other people book cruises. I am sure that if people could deal with the subject of sexuality in a more unbiased way and experience more satisfaction (literally) in this area, there would be fewer wars in the world.. Turning off your brain every now and then and letting yourself be completely captured by this unique erotic atmosphere is an experience that opens your senses and mind in a very special way. It makes you peaceful. It's similar to when we used to go to a big fair when we were kids. I used to get so excited when we went to the big autumn fair at my grandma's house, and I could hardly decide which carousel I wanted to go on first. I feel the same way today at sex clubs and sex parties, only a little bit different in that they are fun fairs for adults. That's why insiders talk about "playing together."

However, I also have to admit that, at the beginning of my sexual research, I experienced one or two moments of culture shock. When you suddenly see things live that you have only imagined all your life, it can be disturbing at first. But this story comes in the next chapter. Here's the prelude: You have to get into this scene first. I mean the noncommercial sex scene, the clubs and parties where swingers, fetish lovers, sadomasochists, and all kinds of other unconventional-thinking people meet. How do you do that if you have no idea what to do, don't know anyone, and you are a woman? First and foremost, you need courage! Munich is a big city, and nowadays we have the internet. Finding out when and where a suitable event is taking place is not that difficult. And you're welcome there, too, especially as a woman. But of course, I didn't know that, and actually going there was a real challenge.

Can you go to a fetish or sadomaso party just like *that*? And alone? As a woman? I could. My curiosity was greater than my fear at that time, as was my desire to finally experience what I had only read about so far. Nothing could hold me back. What I then tracked down first was a fetish party in a Munich disco. My visit to the swingers club with Mr. Darkmind gave me the courage to take the next step. Normal people were there, so I figured it would be the same at this party. They were perhaps dressed a little differently. A strict dress code reigned there: lacquer, leather, latex, rubber, and crazy.

Of course, there are also suitable stores in the big city for this, and I first bought an outfit. I had never entered such a store before; the premiere was Tuesday afternoon. The owner and an employee dressed in black leather were very nice and advised me well; I tried out some things. I finally chose a black latex dress with lace, black patent boots, and a collar. "Well chosen," the owner said. "You'll have a lot of fun at the party. My slave girl and I are coming too." *Aha, he and his slave girl.* I had to smile a little bit. Wow, was I excited now! Four more days!

What actually happens at a fetish party? What can you expect there? Who goes to them? Somehow, everyone has heard of fetishism, but hardly anyone knows what it means in detail. A fetish is generally a focus on an object of sexual desire, that is, something that triggers sexual desire. What you might know is foot fetishism or a soft spot for objects. It can be all sorts of things. Many people perceive certain clothing as a fetish, starting with high heels and nylons and moving on to leather, latex, and rubber. The feeling of tight latex on your skin is already incredible; it's tight and slippery because you sweat like crazy. And that's exactly what makes people horny. The other day a friend forwarded me a link to a community of wool fetishists. These people are turned on by walking around or sleeping in full-body knit suits. It may sound very strange to some, that someone gets horny from wool, falls in love with their rubber ducky, or experiences erotic feelings just looking at metal handcuffs. But unusual sexual preferences are much more widespread than is commonly thought. Unfortunately, there are no statistics or figures on the prevalence of fetishes, but I suspect the number of unreported cases is extremely high! Who will honestly admit to dreaming about diapers, rubber masks, or seventeen-centimeter-high heels? By the way, the same friend who sent me this wool information likes bath foam and anything slippery. I have already organized foam and shower orgies with him. That was something.

At a fetish party, however, it's not so much about the objects of sexual desire; here, the focus is mainly on the clothes. See and be seen, dance, and have fun. Street clothes, jeans, and T-shirts are taboo; only those who prove they have an imagination come in here. The more unusual, the better. LLL, which is shorthand for "lacquer, leather, and latex," is standard. Also, transvestites, drag queens, uniforms, and people with diving goggles and gas masks are also very popular. Actually, it's a bit like a carnival, except that most of the costumes are black or red, shiny, and sometimes deliberately *not* covering important parts of the body. When I went to my first fetish party, I hadn't been so excited in a long time. Well, since the visit to the swingers club, and that was a few months earlier, after all. In the car on the way there, I felt proud. Again, I could fulfill a desire, a longing that I had hidden and suppressed for many years. Now everything was suddenly within my grasp. *What will it be like?* I wondered. *Who will I meet there? What will happen?* I felt brave and inspired. Anticipation is wonderful, and if it is surpassed afterward, it's all the better. I was, of course, much too early, but I found a parking space right in front of the door. I found that I could change clothes on the spot, thank goodness; I did not know whether it was allowed to drive in fetish clothing. I did that later, but that's another topic. I then went in and found that I was, fortunately, not the first. In the locker room, I got to talk to a very nice couple, and after I confessed that I was there for the first time and alone at that, they promised to watch over me for a bit. I could breathe a sigh of relief and slowly relax. All good! There wasn't much going on, but a few characters immediately caught my attention. How ingenious the people were, with the clothes in which they ran around! Flashy, shiny, extraordinary, partly hiding everything, partly so revealing that I could hardly look. Sitting at the bar with my first prosecco in hand, I looked around first in silence, fascinated. And I slowly relaxed. There it was again, this moment when my brain simply switched off, as in meditation. I perceived everything crystal clear; I was wide awake and yet in another world.

Suddenly, a guy came up to me dressed in a leather mask with only his eyes, nostrils, and mouth peeking out, and his leather pants left his butt cheeks exposed. He pressed a small whip into my hand and politely asked me if he could lick my boots while I spanked him. My prosecco almost fell out of my hand, and before I could say yes or no, the guy got down on his knees in front of me, lifted my right foot, and licked the top of my boot. "You have to hit him now," said the woman from the locker room who promised to take care of me. She looked over at me, rather amused. Somewhat awkwardly, I bent down and slapped his bare buttocks. Apparently, the foot licker liked it because he mumbled, "Thank you," and continued licking. It was a funny feeling—I could feel his tongue through the thin boot polish as he slowly worked his way up to my knee. I wouldn't let him go any further. He didn't get to my naked thigh, which would make me uncomfortable. I hit him a little more, more amused than excited, until a very nice, grinning man came up to me and redeemed me. "Hello, I'm Robert!" He ran the sadomasochism (SM) regulars' table in Munich and immediately recognized me as a newcomer. He was curious about who I might be. Women alone at such parties are rare. The conversation with Robert and the rest of the evening were very pleasant and exciting.

"There's not so much gambling going on here," Robert said. "It's more like a party for dancing." That's good, too, and I'm happy to do it. He said that if I wanted to experience more SM, I should go to Kitty, which is a hip club. Robert also invited me to visit the regulars' table. Munich SMers meet there several times a month to chat and exchange everything that has to do with SM. *Sure, I want to go there.* The next meeting would be next week. I saw my bootlicker later at the bar. He didn't take off his mask the whole evening, so I didn't get to see his face. But he gave me a friendly wave while dancing.

I talked to some other people and my curiosity made me want to know everything. I also found a woman who was completely dressed in latex, including boots, a mask, and a thick ruff—exciting. "What do you do when you have to go to the bathroom?" I asked cluelessly. "There's a zipper for that," she tells me. She said she wouldn't take the latex off until the next morning. I assume that's why she jumped into the bathtub because the water was up to her knees.

My conclusion after this evening was, "More of it!" In a unique way, I felt at home among these very modern and open-minded people who lived out their desires so uninhibitedly. It was perfect for the beginning. The next step was to go to Robert's regulars' table and then maybe once to this Kitty club. If there was more to it, I wanted to go there! My curiosity was unstoppable. My mask had fallen. I was not as nice and harmless as I had always thought, and certainly not as well behaved. In these spaces, I felt at home. In places that were anything but moral, people showed their true colors and lived out their desires for dominance, submission, and other erotic preferences.

Perhaps at this point, a small explanation of the term sadomasochism is needed. People who love and practice sadomasochistic types of play are generally called SMers, and all combinations of the various preferences exist. Some like playing with pain, while for others, it doesn't matter at all. Usually, the active one is called a dom, short for *dominant*, and the passive one is called a sub, short for *submissive*. The sadists love to inflict pain on others, and the masochists love when they experience pain themselves. By the way, I quickly learned that masochists don't like going to the dentist any more than other people. The pain must be well-dosed and occur in the right places so that the body's own endorphin release can act like a drug rush and increase pleasure. Creating pain with the appropriate intensity and duration in another person so that he or she can "fly" is a real art. It has to be learned, and it requires great skill and, above all, a lot of attention from the dom. It has nothing at all to do with just banging away. Others are more into playing with dominance and submission. This usually takes place less on a physical level and more on a psychological one. There can be a thrill in controlling another person as well as in relinquishing control completely for once. Dominance and submission are often combined with bondage and inflicting pain, for example, as punishment, which, of course, is staged playfully. All this can also be combined with the use of fetishes, for example, with certain clothing. Bondage, the artistic shackling, has a long tradition in some cultures, including in Japan. It can be learned properly so that it looks very aesthetically pleasing, and the person who is tied up experiences the highest pleasure through it. This must also be done in such a way that the sub's limbs will not fall asleep. Otherwise, the ecstasy is quickly over. There is a huge range of possibilities to live out these inclinations, from being blindfolded to twenty-four-seven, which refers to SM relationships in which the partners live in their roles twenty-four hours a day and seven days a week—constantly.

Some couples draw up real slave contracts in which the do's and don'ts are recorded. However, this has no legal relevance. Personally, I find it difficult to imagine how something like this can be implemented in practice, but I don't need to know that in detail. The important thing is that everything happens in mutual agreement and within a clearly defined framework. Everybody can stop the game at any time. For this, there is a so-called safe word. When the sub says it, the game is over. Often the traffic light variant with green, yellow, and red is used to give the dom a little more leeway. These games work only if both are aroused by it and can enjoy their respective roles. Even if it looks different on the surface, ultimately, the sub is in control because he or she determines the boundaries and rules of the game. The role of sub is also definitely the easier one because he or she usually doesn't have to or can't do much.

This all requires a lot of trust in each other and is rarely practiced in the context of one-night stands, mostly in longer-term relationships. Some people have sadomasochistic fantasies even in childhood. Others come into contact with the subject through a partner. There are hardly any concrete figures about how many people are attracted to these sexual types of play, but the dark figure is also extremely high here. I once read that it is estimated that 10 to 25 percent of the population in industrialized nations have sadomasochistic tendencies. But some say the numbers are between 10 and 90 percent. Don't believe any statistic that you haven't falsified yourself. I am my very own source: If I tell ten friends and acquaintances about something, I may find that three to four look very curious, one grimaces in disgust, and the rest are not interested. Most of the people I have met in this scene, whether men or women, initially became curious about these types of play through a partner and have found that they enjoy it and want more of it. However, it becomes difficult when one discovers this inclination in him- or herself but the partner wants nothing to do with it, as I have also experienced. Then, in the medium term, the question really arises as to if you continue to stay together as a couple while one of you looks for a "play partner," which, by the way, many do; if you would rather turn to a new partner completely; or if you continue to suppress your desires. The last makes little sense. It also makes little sense to want to "convert" a partner who is not curious. As one of my favorite books on this subject says (*The Choice of Agony* by Kathrin Passig and Ira Strübel), "There is not a straight man in every gay man and a butcher in every vegetarian."

What you can do is make your partner curious! Playfully try something new. What would a game that you both enjoy look like?

What Exactly Is BDSM?

We are dealing here with several terms that describe different sexual inclinations. The most common are the terms *sadomasochism, BDSM,* and *bondage*. Most often, people speak collectively of BDSM, an acronym that is composed of the following terms:

- Bondage and discipline (B&D)
- Dominance and submission (D&S)
- Sadism and masochism (S&M)

"Healthy Is What Pleases"

Interview with Dr. Georg G., physician and therapist at one of the largest psychiatric and psychotherapeutic hospitals in Germany

What do doctors and therapists say about SM and fetishes?

As a physician, one sees this from the pathological point of view (i.e., what is pathological and what is not). Fact is sadomasochism and fetishism are listed in the ICD-10 and in the DSM-4. These are the two currently worldwide valid catalogs of criteria for all physical, mental and psychiatric diseases. Sadism and masochism are considered pathological in the DSM-4 if practiced without the partner's consent ("nonconsenting") or lead to considerable suffering in oneself or to social problems. Actually, this means that as long as one does such things consensually and of one's own free will, all is well. Unfortunately, this is often not yet understood in practice.

Are there catalogs of sexual deviancy? What else does it say?

In Germany, we work primarily with the ICD-10, published by the WHO. Under chapter F65, one finds various disorders of sexual preference, so-called paraphilias. This list does not directly say anything about whether one is ill or not but merely describes the various phenomena and categorizes them. It should also be noted that this classification is not exactly up to date but is based on assessments made by the German psychiatrist and forensic pathologist Richard von Krafft-Ebing in 1886. His work *Psychopathia Sexualis* was the first to summarize everything that was considered "not normal" during sex. At that time, oral sex, masturbation, and homosexuality were also included among sexual disorders. One would think that a lot has changed since then. Homosexuality was, by the way, only deleted from the ICD-10 as a disease in 1991!

Where is the line between "boringly normal" and "grossly abnormal"? Is there one at all?

The boundaries are fluid. And they are not determined by doctors, but from my point of view by society on the one hand and by the person himself on the other. I would put it this way: For a person, sexuality is pathological when it has pathological value for him or her (i.e., when he or she suffers from it). This can be because they are unfulfilled desires or because these desires cause problems in everyday life, in social life, in finding a partner, or even in the relationship with the partner. Possibly, sexual urges can also have forensic effects, which means getting into trouble with the law or simply that they are not socially accepted in any way. For example, pedophilia was more or less normal in ancient Rome. If you read stories about some emperors, they were often attracted to young boys, and it wasn't outlawed back then. The ancient Greeks are also known for their love for boys. Nowadays, that's about the most outlawed sexual deviation there is.

For a good reason!

Yes, of course. But you can see that this is ultimately determined by society. There are virtually no contact points for people with pedophilic tendencies, and they themselves suffer the most because they don't know how they can get rid of their pressure or who they can even ask for help. Of course, they can go to the doctor and get treatment, but the doctor may then come into conflict with the duty of confidentiality. It can be treated psychotherapeutically or with medication, and the urge is then curbed. A very sensitive subject.

Not everywhere. I once read about primitive people where the boys are introduced to adulthood and learn sexuality by serving the older boys sexually—as an initiation, so to speak.

I haven't heard that yet, but it could be; it's such an issue with the rites of passage. In our country, boys are given a hundred dollars at the age of eighteen so that they can go to a brothel for the first time. After all, that is only determined by society.

Let's stay with SM for a moment. What is still normal there? Some are already afraid when they let themselves be blindfolded; others let themselves be tied up and beaten until they have bruises.

It always depends: Do I suffer from it or the other person or does the partnership suffer from it? This can already happen when the other person doesn't want to participate and rejects my wishes, for example, to hit me. Then I have a problem because I can't live out the urge. The border to the pathological is reached where the whole thing causes problems either for myself or my partner or in my social life. Otherwise, everything that two people do with each other, who both want to do it, is normal, and that can be anything. Therefore, the basic rule in the SM area is always: safe, sane, and consensual!

I think that if you act out your urges in the right place, that is even actively healthy. Suppressing them, on the other hand, makes you sick.

In any case, the suppression of drives causes problems. According to Sigmund Freud, behaviors that deviate from the norm are due to unresolved conflicts and problems in early childhood development—for example, a failure to resolve the Oedipus complex in the oedipal phase.

Um, what exactly is the oedipal phase?

This takes place between the fourth and sixth years of life. As a boy, you are first in love with your mother, then you experience your father as a rival; Oedipus, in the classic saga, even killed him. Motherly love is a huge issue. According to Freud, such deviations occur if this conflict is not resolved, for example, if the boy does not detach himself from the mother and identify with the father. Love is so strong that it always finds a way, no matter how unusual.

Are there also newer approaches? Maybe these are not aberrations at all but simply natural desires: A person with a lot of strength and testosterone might just like to hit something.

Freud's teaching is still very relevant in many ways. He says, for example, that in every human being, all the predispositions and potentials are present, and the so-called superego tries to maintain a balance throughout life, depending on the society in which a person grows up and how he is brought up. Some drives that do not conform to society are suppressed at a very early age. For example, according to Freud, everyone has a homosexual drive within them, but it is not socially accepted, so the superego suppresses it again.

Hmm, then one could almost assume that in societies where it is accepted, there are more homosexuals and "perverts"?

In our country, you really do get that impression. At least more and more people dare to admit it because they no longer have to fear being ostracized by society and losing their jobs, for example. In the area of SM, however, this is still very subliminal. If you take a closer look at how often SM topics appear in films, how often women are shown tied up or someone is taken away in handcuffs, locked up and beaten ... then these topics are actually visible everywhere. After all, they seem to occupy the imagination of a great many people and arouse their interest. In the Middle Ages, people were publicly tortured in the marketplace, and everyone watched; those were really big events.

Can sex make you healthy, even if it is not "normal"?

One thing is clear in any case: If you suppress sexual urges, that does not make you healthy because they will break some way, either by suffering from it and eventually becoming physically ill or by finding substitute solutions that are not successful, which is then called neuroses. Roughly speaking, a neurosis is an attempt to solve problems with a bad method.

What are typical neuroses?

The best known are anxiety disorders, such as fear of large places, crowds, confined spaces, and spiders. Neuroses also include compulsive acts, such as compulsive washing or hypochondria. Hysteria also falls under it, or used to fall under it. Today, it no longer exists officially. It was removed from the catalog, labeled and classified according to the predominant symptom, and listed under neurotic and stress disorders. Here I have to come back to Freud. He saw "perversion" as the negative of neurosis because of the direct satisfaction of drives. It means something like this: A perversion is the opposite of a neurosis. Interesting, isn't it?

When practicing SM, do people put things at risk?

I think it starts way before that. Many people are afraid that they will ruin their relationship if they even bring up something like that. If you approach your partner with an unusual wish, it requires a lot of effort, and I think most people prefer not to say it at all. This is not a special SM topic but a general problem in partnerships that wishes are not expressed. You don't talk about it and remain unsatisfied inside. Under certain circumstances, this also destroys the emotional, interpersonal connection between two partners.

If one then dares and the other wants to join in, what do you have to look out for?

The fear is much greater than the actual danger of physically breaking something. You usually feel your way forward slowly. For example, hands falling asleep from being tied up happens more often than not. However, this is not so much due to the restraint itself but more to the position of the arms. I'm sure everyone has experienced this: If you put your arms over your head for a longer period of time in a recliner or fold them behind your head, they will fall asleep at some point. But they wake up again as soon as you change the position and move them! Hands falling asleep are simply a warning sign of the body; if you pay attention to these "first warning signs," there are no problems.

And if you want to go further?

Most of the injuries you deal with in the SM area are harmless and heal on their own, for example, bruises, redness, or small abrasions. This is no worse than normal everyday injuries. If you consult with your partner and also communicate repeatedly during the session, they usually don't occur at all, or if they do, they are intentional. For some, a red butt has a very special appeal. As a rule, SM users are even rather overcautious, which, from my point of view, is very good. The most important thing is to discuss the limits with your partner and observe them during the game. This can sometimes be a bit difficult in the heat of the moment. But that's what the safe word is for. You agree on a word, and if someone says it, it's over immediately.

Does that mean there is no risk of boundaries being crossed?

This kind of sexuality requires a lot of sensitivity. It can happen when unexpected emotional outbursts occur or you suddenly realize that the boundary is different today than it was yesterday. Then you break off the session or do something else and talk about it. This does not cause any permanent damage. As I said, the basic requirement is always that the game takes place by mutual agreement and that you communicate with each other and trust each other.

You yourself have already had experience with the dominant role.

As far as I can remember, the thoughts were always there. I then came up with it concretely through a partner. Just for fun, I once held her hands together behind her back in bed. She enjoyed it and asked me if I would like to tie her up. I did it!

What was that like for you?

Incredibly beautiful. A great and exciting experience to see the woman so helpless and at the same time so excited. We then slowly developed this, first with the bathrobe belt, and then became more professional, bought handcuffs, tried out all sorts of things, and integrated them into the relationship. We both thought that was great. After that, I had a partner who didn't want that at first. She thought I didn't love her anymore but only saw her as a sex object. I let the subject rest and held her gently by the hands only once during sex. I noticed that she enjoyed that, and then I tried the bathrobe belt at some point. We slowly approached it, and she actually really enjoyed it. She said herself that she had much more intense climaxes when tied up.

Bondage has a long tradition in some countries.

In Japan, for example, bondage art is socially accepted and almost ubiquitous, for example, in the mangas, the Japanese comics. But also in nightclubs, literature, pictures, and everywhere, you encounter this topic. The Japanese place a lot of emphasis on visuals and put a lot of effort into it. You can take courses in artistic bondage, and there are famous teachers. Bondage serves the presentation and accessibility of the woman in a sexual way. The

American says "access." And, of course, it also serves to positively emphasize the woman's body and give her pleasure.

Bondage feels really cool too.

Some women have already reported to me that their orgasms become stronger through bondage. This is due to the more intense body tension that they can build up in bondage. Women often hold onto the bed rail shortly before orgasm or claw into the mattress to build up tension. Tied up, this works even better.

Did you continue to research the topic together?

Yes, and she has increasingly enjoyed it. I then also left her tied up in the apartment once and went briefly to the bakery; we both found that very exciting and arousing.

What is it exactly that turns you on? Can you describe it?

On one hand, of course, the excitement of the woman. And on the other hand, I have control. The woman simply can't help herself in this situation; she can't get away, can't defend herself, and is at the mercy of others. Seeing and feeling this helplessness turns me on. Well, it is, of course, ultimately the case that the woman has the power in this game because she determines what I can and cannot do, what excites her and what does not. For me, it's the theme of "The Beautiful Prisoner." There is even a picture with this title, by René Magritte.

Do you find that somehow pathological?

Not at all. Otherwise, I would probably get treatment.... (Laughs) I don't suffer from it in any way.

And have you always found suitable partners?

Yes, I have been able to incorporate that into every partnership so far. Often it was for the woman's first contact with bondage and SM, and I introduced women to this subject. They liked it; I never forced anyone to do anything.

Being a "sub" is also a great experience: giving up control and not knowing what the other person is doing but at the same time being safe and feeling the certainty that one's limits will be accepted.

Everything that happens is done by mutual consent and for mutual pleasure increase. After all, the game takes place within a certain framework, and this is clearly communicated. The dom never does anything against the will of the sub. This requires a lot of trust and attentiveness. The sub gives up control and runs the risk of the dom overstepping the boundaries a little bit in the process. This is exactly what gives an extra kick, and in the process, one's own limits are also explored. After the blow, the sub can always say stop, but then the blow is already over, and at that moment, the own limit has already been expanded.

In your estimation, are there more dominant people or more submissive people?

From my experience and the relevant forums and circles, I would say that there are more subs, certainly among men. The demand for dominant women far exceeds the supply. Also, at the parties, as a dominant woman, you are the most desired one. There are also many submissive women who don't find it easy to come out. There are often fears that boundaries will be crossed, that they will be hurt, or are too much at the mercy of others.

I also tried myself once in the dominant role. You play with the body of the other much like you play an instrument.

You have to tune in exactly to the other person; you are the active part. You have to know and feel the boundaries, and at the same time, you have to explore them. This is a role play, and you have to come up with something. It's not enough to tie the other person to the bed; there has to be more. It's a bit like a craft that you can keep refining. The role as a sub is easier—you don't have to worry about anything, you are the center of attention, everything revolves around you, and you can completely let yourself go and enjoy.

Have you tried the passive role yourself?

Honestly, no. It is appealing from the idea, but it is very hard to find resourceful dominant women. Many women have inhibitions about using restraints or whips.

At the time, I found it particularly difficult to make clear and tough announcements to the man in the game. But that's also a good exercise for the rest of my life.

Yes, in any case. (Laughs) Not many women can do that, and the ones who can do it really well usually earn very good money doing it.

What was your most exciting SM experience? Were there situations in which you experienced a very special thrill, or do you have that every time?

I actually always have it. It's different every time, so there's no routine. At most, there are variations and some things that I particularly like. For example, going for a walk in the park with a woman tied up under her coat. The nice thing is I decide what we do.

You've also worked in the emergency room yourself many times. You hear the wildest stories about sex accidents.

Occasionally people come in with pinched nerves due to clumsy and too tight restraints, for example, with handcuffs, then sometimes the thumb becomes a little numb. However, this heals on its own after a few days, so all it takes is a little education on what to look out for in the future. What also happens is that the penis is injured by objects that are not intended for this purpose. There I must say, household objects and genitals just don't go together in most cases! The most famous example is the legendary doctoral thesis about penis injuries by vacuum cleaners.

I once heard that the classic is foreign bodies that disappear in the intestine.

The anus is a very erogenous zone, and it's a lot of fun to play with it. However, even that should only be done with toys that are designed for that purpose. As the name suggests, the sphincter muscle has the task of closing quite tightly. And it does not easily release objects that you put in it. The toys available for sale in this area have special provisions, whether it's a long cord to pull them out again or a plate or thickening that prevents the item from slipping all the way in. Household items or even a vibrator, which is intended for use in or on the vagina, do not meet this requirement!

Finally, a very topical issue: Does burnout also have to do with sexuality that is not lived?

I can't back this up scientifically, but I would definitely say that there is a connection. Burnout has to do primarily with a work-life balance that doesn't work. If things aren't right in your private life, you generally don't have sex. And if the balance is missing, the overload becomes greater and greater. In addition, burnout can be both a symptom and a trigger of depression, and that's about the worst sex killer. When you're depressed, you don't feel like having sex.

Do physical or psychological causes play a role in displeasure?

In women, lack of desire is more likely to be psychological; in men, both occur. As a rule, they first see a urologist, and if everything is in order physically and organically, they look for psychological causes. What few know: There are some drugs that are prescribed today and taken by many that have a significant impact on erectile function. First and foremost are antidepressants, which have now become almost "lifestyle drugs." There are first variants of drugs with weaker side effects, but in principle, all can have such an effect. We have higher stresses at work and often, in our private lives, we feel worse and have less sex. Then we take the pill and feel better again, but we still don't feel like having sex because the medication prevents that. And then we're frustrated again. Sexual problems are a big topic, but very few people address it directly because it's naturally very unpleasant.

Once again, back to society: nowadays, it is possible to earn a lot of money with an exhibitionist inclination in our country.

The boundaries of what is socially accepted are becoming more and more blurred. There is a lady, a former porn nude model, who has become famous because she appears more or less naked in public, whether at parties, press events, or autograph sessions in shopping malls. We would immediately report a guy who walks around naked in the park. Well, except maybe in Munich at the Eisbach in the nudist zone.

There are also societies in which everything to do with sexuality is much more strictly regulated than here in our country.

In some Arab countries, women go swimming with a veil. Showing oneself naked in any place is strictly forbidden. Even in the swimming pool! No joke: Muslim women wear full-body bathing suits called "burkini."

Thank you for the riveting conversation!

Chapter 6
FAVORITE FANTASY

**Implementing them means entering
uncharted territory because you have no
idea what will happen if you do.**

There is magic in every beginning.

— Hermann Hesse

IT TOOK ME A FEW years to come to terms with myself and to admit
who I am and what I like. And it took a few people accompanying
me on this path; it's something people usually can't do alone. It
is incredibly relieving and maybe even the most important thing
you can achieve in life. Be yourself and show yourself as you are.
If you, as a man, love many women, stand by it! If you are really
authentic, you will find a suitable partner who accepts that. If you, as
a woman, like men *and* women, tell your partner that. The chances
are extremely good that he will also like it! I like to be around people
who are openly gay or lesbian or bisexual, for example, because they
are so incredibly, pleasantly relaxed and easygoing.

But how do you get started? As a coach, I would say to stop
rolling things around in your head and get to work, step by step.
What's the problem with trying something new with your partner?

Surprise him! If you don't have a partner, why don't you start with yourself? The more clearly you know what you want and who you are, the more likely you will be to find someone suitable. If you are bored with your life, how can anyone else find you interesting? Men have a harder time than women. As a woman, you only need to go out once and you can at least choose a sex partner. Men are not as fortunate. Consider this: in a very exciting experiment run by an American university, psychologist Elaine Hatfield arranged for students to ask opposite-sex, good-looking fellow students on campus the following questions:

1. Would you go out with me tonight?
2. Would you go to bed with me tonight?

The results were clear: 75 percent of the men asked would enter into a relationship with a woman to go to bed with her, and 50 percent would go out with her. Conversely, 56 percent of women would go out with a man who asked, but not a single one would go to bed with him. Please do not despair; you just have to try a little harder.

Back to the favorite fantasy: Now, let's get down to business and no more excuses! Because even if you have a partner, it's not necessarily easier. For something new to happen in your life, you need a coincidence (what you have no control over), a high threshold for suffering, or a huge portion of curiosity—and possibly another person to take you by the hand. Preferably, you would have all at once. And fear is always involved because you have no idea what happens when you enter new territory. If you hold on to everything you know and don't move out of your familiar box called the comfort zone, there will be no room for anything new.

The real fun is outside the box and also during sex.

When did you have your most brilliant sexual experiences? What did you have to give up so that something new could come into your life? What fear did you have to overcome? Or was it easy? Why?

The nice thing is, once you get going, it gets easier. It was definitely like that with me. I had dared to go to a swingers club with a stranger and to a fetish party alone. A little less than a year after my first Life Changing Sex with the master baker, I became even bolder. I wanted to explore my dark side further, specifically my fantasies of being bound and tied up and losing control and letting go, which had been floating around in my head for many years. It was clear to me that, in order to delve further into this world, I needed to meet the right people who knew about this kind of thing and with whom I wasn't embarrassed. I had to drop some more of my masks, especially the "I-always-have-everything-under-control-and-that's-good mask." At the SMIGO regulars' table, I met nice people to talk to, which gave me incredible courage. They also had the best tips for parties, shops, and just about anything a newbie would want to know. Robert was someone I could confide in about anything, and we hit it off right away. Mr. Darkmind would have been a suitable partner for me to delve further into the dark world, but apparently, I was not for him. Shortly after our meeting, he fell in love with another woman, and I continued my search. I started to bustle around on special internet forums about sadomasochism, registered on an SM dating site, and placed an ad with the following text:

Neugierige, ungebundene Frau, Akademikerin, beruflich engagiert und erfolgreich, 33 Jahre, 1,63m groß, schlank, voller Energie, möchte lange gehegte Leidenschaft ausleben, mit einem ebenbürtigen Mann, der Intelligenz und Dominanz ausstrahlt, der keine Dauersklavin sucht, sondern erotische Momente, und der bereit ist, eine Anfängerin in die Abgründe der Lust zu begleiten. Der beiderseitige Spaß steht im Vordergrund, wenn mehr draus wird, habe ich nichts dagegen. Ich bin „echt", Freaks und Fakes keine Chance.

(Curious, unattached woman, academic, professionally committed and successful, 33 years, 1.63 m tall, slim, full of energy, would like to live out long cherished passion with an equal man who radiates intelligence and dominance, who is not looking for a permanent slave, but an erotic moment, and who is willing to accompany a beginner into the abysses of pleasure. The mutual fun

is in the foreground; if more becomes of it, I have nothing against it. I am "real" and freaks and fakes no chance.)

Over sixty responses arrived in the following weeks in my mailbox, ranging from really sympathetic, human, and pleasant to things like, "Hi slave! I would like to devote myself to your education," which amused me more than stimulated me. Very many were in fixed relationships and were only looking for the game. Some were probably more lonely. Every type was there, from very attractive to "does not go out at all." I had rarely read so many humorous emails until then. I met some of them for coffee, at a Greek restaurant, in a vegetarian restaurant, and for a walk. And finally, with one of them, there was a spark. He wrote me under the subject "Fun":

> Hello -
> I am also real, live in MUC, my name is Paul and
> I would be happy if you would introduce yourself.
> The weekend is just around the corner, and the sun
> is shining :-) The best conditions - so get in touch; I
> look forward to it. Many greetings Paul

With Paul—who in truth is not called that at all, as he later revealed to me—a very nice communication developed. He was somehow unobtrusive compared to most of the others, who either tried to present themselves as particularly empathetic and understanding of women or as dominant super-machos. Paul seemed relaxed; he was not looking for anything special and did not write much, but what he wrote made sense.

We arranged to meet for dinner two weeks after the first mail contact. He didn't talk much, but I liked him. I would confide in him. The very next day, we met at my apartment for the first time for a "session" (that's what insiders call it; you could also call it a playdate).

I know it's not a good idea to invite a strange man to my home right away, especially not if I intend to let him tie me up. In the scene, there is a very simple safety rule for this: You arrange with a friend to make a phone call at a certain time. If the phone call is not made, the friend is alerted that there may be problems. This is called covering. I relied on my knowledge of human nature, as I did with the master baker. It was just right. Who else should I have called? No one knew what I was up to, and that was just fine. I knew my friends and acquaintances would all throw their hands up in horror and try to dissuade me. I didn't feel like doing that. I just trusted, and it worked out. Paul came to me right on time with a bag full of toys, handcuffs, a small whip, a gag, and some more. He didn't talk much—he never did—but he tried everything on me little by little, and I let it happen.

We didn't have sex; we just played. It's hard to describe how that felt to me. To surrender myself to a stranger, with whom I had just had a single vegetarian meal and about whom I knew almost nothing else, was already borderline. Borderline brilliant! The cocktail of fear, curiosity, and lust was overwhelming. *What will he do next?* I kept wondering. I left the choreography to him and just got involved. I had this incredible feeling of having my hands tied and simply not having to do anything and not knowing or deciding what happens next. I didn't have to do anything; I just felt and enjoyed. Experiencing something you've dreamed about for many years for real can be quite exhilarating. I didn't turn my head off completely, not that first night. I always told him what I liked and what I didn't, and we were in communication the whole time.

The safe word we established was *sunflower.* I didn't need it, though. Paul would probably have been satisfied with the handcuffs for this first session, but I wanted to try out everything he had with him. How does a gag feel or an anal plug? What creates a shiver, and what might be unspectacular after all? I could not get enough. After three hours, we were through. The SM session was exhausting for both of us. When he left my apartment, it was clear to me: Again, it had been such a day after whose end nothing would be as it had been before because something fundamental had changed. A fantasy had become a reality—a new form of Life Changing Sex.

Two days later, Paul was at my door again and came regularly over the next few weeks. We never talked much; it wasn't even necessary. He came, we had fun, then he left again. Something I could never have imagined before was having a purely sexual affair with a man. With Paul, I learned to do it. He didn't want a relationship, and it was okay. Our deal was different: having fun without commitment and being together without talking. It just worked for us. For the first time, I experienced that a sexual encounter—I'll just call it that now—between two people can vary so much and really be different every time. From my long-term relationship, I knew that most everything runs more or less in the same pattern. There are a few different positions, foreplay, main act, credits, and maybe different places, and that's it.

SMers refer to people who have "normal sex" as *vanillas,* as in vanilla ice cream. It comes in different varieties, but it always remains vanilla ice cream. How about pistachio or chocolate?

I found it particularly exciting to work with Paul. He always texted me beforehand and told me how I should prepare, like put on my collar, take off my underwear, and little things that were extremely effective in this context. He had a lot of imagination, and we tried a lot of things. Some of what he wanted was too hard for me, some just didn't turn me on, but most of it was just awesome. With Paul, I was allowed to be a woman, a lover, and a sex object, and he desired me. My job, my everyday life—all that was irrelevant. It did not interest him. I didn't have to represent anyone anymore; I was just me with my lust, and bit by bit, I learned to let myself go. I still remember well one Thursday at the end of May when he came to me again and smacked me—or rather, my backside. I'm not really into spanking, but that evening with him, I went for it, and we both had a lot of fun. The next day I flew to Berlin for a convention. I didn't notice anything else except that I couldn't get rid of the men at the bar in the evening. Apparently, they were quite fascinated by me. I must have radiated something; something was different. I wanted to spend the second evening of the convention comfortably in the hotel sauna, so I took my clothes off, put my bathrobe on, and headed off to the wellness section. By chance, I looked in the mirror while changing and dropped the towel in shock. My backside was covered with small green and blue bruises. They didn't hurt, but they were pretty obvious. A whole new feeling came over me; I was stunned, smiling, and excited. Paul had managed to give me a striking reminder of him on my journey after all. He was crazy. And so was I, I suppose. I went to the sauna anyway, hiding behind my towel. Only a few other guests were there.

Once, Paul and I exchanged roles. He was a so-called switcher, so he loved both the dominant and the submissive roles. As a dominatrix, I was still a bit helpless at that time. It didn't really turn me on either, but it was still an exciting experience that I was to savor more extensively four years later. So I spent the summer of 2006 with this unusual affair, which above all felt unusually good to me. There was much to discover, and every meeting was different and new.

Parallel to the affair with Paul, I naturally continued looking around for men because I was looking for a committed relationship again. Among the many responses to my ad, there was no suitable candidate, and subconsciously I probably didn't want to commit myself yet. So I first continued to research and did what aroused my greatest curiosity and what I also had quite a bit of respect for at the same time.

I paid a visit to Kitty, Munich's hottest sadomaso club (which unfortunately no longer exists). Robert from the SM regulars' table invited me to celebrate his birthday there and quickly found a nice companion for me among the SM friends, Daniel. He was nice and uncomplicated, a few years younger than me, and experienced in the scene. I could confide in him. I had only very vague ideas about how it might look there and what awaited me. I already had a mental image of the swingers club, but an SM club was certainly something else.

Daniel picked me up, and I was excited to wear my black latex dress again. For him, it was clear: We go there already in the outfits. It was high summer, warm enough, and he said he would walk around occasionally in that outfit.

When he was then standing in front of my door wearing a green military suit and holding an arsenal of handcuffs and other toys, *If my neighbors see me now* ... flashed through my mind. Again, I was in for an evening in which I did not know at all what awaited me, and again, I got this exciting, tingling, pressing feeling in the belly. Today, it would happen. I would enter a place where people could give space to all their fantasies—something I had dreamed of so often and something I had longed for so often. Even many years ago, when I still lived with my husband in Cologne, I used to secretly read articles about orgies, wild parties, and clubs like this one. But I never had the opportunity or the courage to experience something like them for real. In the meantime, I had found the right people who had very similar thoughts, desires, and concerns as I did, people I could confide in. They were sexually open, modern, free, like-minded people. Today was to be the day. And again, with a man I hardly knew. Already when going in, I noticed that my mind went to screensaver mode. I can't help it. When this happens, I am only in the here and now. Suddenly, I see everything in 3D, whereas it two-dimensional and flat before. I dive back into this other world.

Since we are very early at the Kitty, I first get an extensive tour from Daniel. Tied up, of course. I am incredibly excited; Disneyland has nothing on it. We went through the many rooms, called playrooms: the dark catacombs; the men's salon with cage, billiard table, and bulky leather chairs; the couples room with black leather couches, a large latex-covered bed, a love swing, and the bar by the large dance floor. I devoured everything with hungry looks. I cannot get enough. And yet there were hardly any people there. For the birthday toast with Robert, Daniel freed me briefly from my handcuffs. When I had to go to the bathroom, he locked them again and accompanied me, watching me through the open door. It took a lot of getting used to. I was a little ashamed, I must admit, but I didn't care, if he enjoys it.

Little by little, some of Robert's guests and many other clubbers trickled in. I was drunk from the many impressions and from the fancy clothes; there is a strict dress code, as there was at the fetish party. The people were crazily made up and had plenty of tattoos and piercings decorating their bodies. And their faces ranged from happy to enraptured, and all were wide awake. Most of them felt like I did; they loved being there in this melting pot of possibilities, where people drop all masks. I had the feeling that, there, I could let go and be who I really am.

Finally! The first ones started their sessions, quite publicly. Anyone who wanted to could watch. In the big room, a pretty woman was tied to a St. Andrew's cross. Next to it, a man in a maid's costume was being whipped; in the clinic room, a naked woman was strapped to a gynecologist's exam table; next door, wax was being dripped on a hairy man's back. I could not avert my eyes. I was fascinated and repulsed at the same time, lust mixed with horror. These sights were almost too hard for me, and my eyes were huge. I believe it's called culture shock.

Spellbound, I watched where a man who had only one arm beat his wife as she lay humbly on a trestle. She must have been a singer because her screams were very sonorous. At some point, she started to sing an aria as if she were still cheering him on—grotesque, crazy. A whole crowd formed around the two of them. I almost couldn't look anymore, wincing every time I heard the rhythmic slapping of the paddle on her bare butt. Daniel stood next to me and grinned contentedly. Later, I saw the opera singer sitting in one of the thick leather chairs. The look on her face revealed peace, happiness, satisfaction. Slightly enraptured and grateful, she smiled at her partner and sipped a glass of red wine. Madness.

Should I have a guilty conscience? Am I doing something forbidden or wrong? Am I allowed to be here and observe these people? Above all, may I feel pleasure in doing so? These questions crept around in my head. I, too, am still influenced by morals, although I always thought that none of this was any of my business anymore. But it isn't. What I saw and experienced that evening, you just don't do! Or do you? Who decides that?

I don't think anyone is indifferent to something like that. Some people might find it disgusting and want nothing to do with it. It's also good to know that. I would never have guessed all the different ways people can shiver with pleasure when others feel nothing at all or everything passes them by. How different we are! Anyway, it's my thing, not that I have to experience it all myself. I'm not into pain, as I mentioned before. But in this atmosphere, with the dimly lit rooms, the passion of the people who give themselves over to their lust without inhibitions, and the loud booming trance-inducing music, everyone is allowed to be complete as he or she is. And everyone is! That's what fascinates me about it.

Someone with a full-body latex suit, gas mask, and giant rubber tits who sits at the bar watching all evening and whose actual sex is indeterminate is just as welcome as the scrawny older white-haired guy who wears nothing at all except a neon-colored ring around his testicles and black loafers with socks. What a collection of weirdos who, in normal life, are probably perfectly unremarkable good citizens—clerks, officials, secretaries. They have found their channel through which they can express who they really are. I wonder, *When are they actually in disguise? Here or there?*

Daniel and I drank a prosecco at the bar. And for me, it was clear: I wanted more of it! Not every day and not every week. But I had decided that my favorite fantasies should no longer remain dreams and I wanted to explore my dark side further. Piece by piece, I would conquer the desire and then experience and feel what had previously been only in my head. Now, the fun really begins!

I have found my playground.

Chapter 7

SURRENDER INSTEAD
OF BRAIN JERKING

**Many pieces of advice do not make us happy
but selfish. Love has to do with devotion;
whores know that better than saints. And "love
yourself" is nicely meant but wrongly thought.
It should be said, "Open your heart"!**

DURING MY RESEARCH JOURNEY THROUGH sexuality, I have questioned and looked anew at many things that I had previously considered to be true. It is two completely different things to read about something and hear and experience it from a third-party perspective compared to actually experiencing it yourself. After all, you're bombarded with advice everywhere, especially if you're a single woman in her midthirties who still wants children, because that was—besides all the trying out and exploring of my sexual fantasies—also an important topic for me. Only how should that fit together now? Sure, children come from sex, just not necessarily from the type I was trying out. And I must say, finding a man of a suitable age who is interested in SM, is free, and still wants children seemed to me nearly impossible. I had several relationships, but something always did not fit.

Maybe there is actually something to this alleged study that says a woman around forty is statistically more likely to be struck by a meteorite than to find a man who wants to have children with her. Yes, you really do wonder about things like that. What I then also encountered, again and again, were tips on the subject of self-love. According to the motto, you have to love yourself first before someone else can do it. Self-love is preached to us in all spiri-, eso-, and other life-help-guides. And it is a big trap. Because as it was originally meant, it is unfortunately rarely understood. Superficially it sounds logical and somehow also good. It's a thousand times easier to think *I'm great* than to get someone else to do it. And a little self-love can't hurt, after all. Can it? Except, perhaps, in that it creates enormous pressure. I know what I'm talking about; I've been desperately single long enough and I've sucked up all these books. I hugged myself every day and mumbled, "I love me, I love me, I love me, I love me," and generally expected my dream man to finally come around the corner. I have always visualized how much I like myself, thought up all kinds of rituals, and wondered how I could love myself even more. Guys, this is all only in the head and has nothing to do with the reality! And accordingly, "he" did not come. Instead, the pressure grew, as did the guilty conscience that I still did not love myself enough.

The fact is that I was constantly surrounded by all kinds of nice men whom I didn't even notice because of all the self-love. And the more I visualized my dream partner, wrote down all his qualities, and sent wishes to the universe, the greater the pressure became. But the solution is quite simple: *Stop with the futile theory!* Give your head a break and open your heart!

Fortunately, you can do that for anyone, Prince Charming or not, and it always helps because you take the focus off your own needs. Almost no one talks or writes about the real crucial point in love, sex, and relationships. People who are in long-term relationships know what I mean. A good relationship has to do with *not* being preoccupied with yourself. It happens when one loves the other more than oneself and is in service of the other.

The thought, *I must first love myself,* has a fundamental error.

As long as I revolve around myself, I am anything but attractive to someone else. Who wants to deal with a self-absorbed egomaniac or a prudish egomaniac who knows exactly what he or she wants (and doesn't want)? A really good relationship comes from asking, "What am I willing to give?" instead of the eternal "What do I need?"

Looking back, it was a very interesting time, and I learned a lot about myself and other people. When you start to really deal with a topic, you suddenly encounter many completely different opinions, advice, and even dogmas, and everyone thinks they know what is good for you. The art is to find your own truth in confusion. In sex, I became more and more free; in love, I still needed some coaching. Surrender instead of brain jerking.

"Are you ready to do everything for a man for half a year so that he can make it big and become successful and happy without expecting anything in return yourself?" A very well-meaning person once asked me this question, and it shocked me at the time. How would you answer it?

It is the same with sex. If you always want to have something or receive something—tenderness, security, satisfaction, whatever—that seems quickly selfish and overwhelms potential partners. The magic word is *curiosity*: People who start to be curious about their partners and, first of all, want to fulfill their wishes and to see what the other person needs, experience something new, a new dimension. For this, they must open their hearts, direct their attention away from themselves, and give it to their partners and their needs. Then something great is possible, and self-love arises naturally at the same time. *It should not be "Love yourself" but "Open your heart."*

Here's a mind game: Try paying attention to your partner's needs during sex for one month and focus on making him or her happy, no matter how you feel at the moment or what you feel like doing. Can you imagine? Is one month way too long? Okay, how long could you keep it up? Maybe two weeks? Or one?

You might think that's what you've been doing all along anyway. You always do everything for *her*, do exactly what she wants, have sex only when Madam feels like it, or you have sex at all only because *he* wants it, you have no need for it yourself, and if it does not work at all, well, then you just let it pass over you *for him*.

No, dear readers, that is not what I mean. I mean something completely different. I mean real service to your partner. I mean that you really do what the other person wishes from the bottom of his or her heart. You are there for them and you completely surrender to their wishes and have fun doing it. This idea surely puts many, especially women, out of sorts. *"He* should please first respond to *my* wishes!"* No, it's the other way around! Good sex begins with service. Try it out for a month. And if that is too much for you: At Tantra, there is an exercise called the King's Game. There, one fulfills all of the other's wishes for one evening without wanting anything themselves, and that lasts a few hours at most. (This is described in more detail on page 94.)

For those who are at a loss and don't know exactly how to go about it, here are some instructions:

If you are a woman, your man loves your femininity and everything that goes with it: your hair, your smile, your breasts, your pussy, your carefree nature, your spontaneity, your devotion, your sweetness, your reactions to what he does to you, that you squirm, that you moan, that you love what he does, and that you are a woman. If you give him that, he will be happy. Your main job is simply to have fun during sex!

If you are a man, your woman loves your masculinity and everything that goes with it: your strength, your strong hands, your decisiveness, your fighting spirit, but also your ability to adjust to her wishes and do what makes her happy, your ability to drive her crazy with your lovemaking skills. Your main job during sex is simply to give your partner fun!

Speaking of service, most men love to be in service for women, from holding doors to cleaning while naked. Girls, give the guys more chances to do those things!

On the subject of service, I conducted a very interesting interview with a woman who worked as a prostitute for a year and got to know the subject of sex from a completely different perspective. Here are her most important insights from this job, which is generally considered so questionable.

"Women can learn to have an orgasm at any time."
Interview with Bianca S., an amateur prostitute

"If you learn to surrender, you can have an orgasm at any time. And if you open your heart, it doesn't matter with which man," says Bianca, a young woman in her late twenties. She is a friend of mine who worked as a prostitute in a Munich massage studio for a year. Bianca is so different from what most would imagine a whore to be. I was very happy that she answered my probing questions. Bianca has mastered "squirting," or the "female cum." This is very popular with men because only a few women can do it and only if they actually have an orgasm. We met in the German railway lounge at Munich's main train station. They serve very tasty latte macchiatos, and talking about such an unusual topic among all the travelers and businesspeople was fun for both of us.

Bianca, when we met in 2008, you were a housewife and mother and worked for a telephone company on the side. And you did martial arts.

I have always been very curious and have tried out a lot. (Laughs) What I've always loved is riding motorcycles, and I'm also a very physical person. Yes, I learned martial arts back then. Taekwondo class was the first time I learned how to feel every single millimeter of my body. Martial arts was just the thing for me at that time to develop myself and to really connect with my body.

You then took part in a porn film production. How did you get there? What made you curious?

I went on auditions because I wanted to work as a model. A producer hired me, and I was completely fascinated when I visited his studio. I had to fill out a questionnaire about what I would do, including erotic photos or (partial) nudes or filming. I didn't tick off all that at that time. The producer first took normal photos of me. Initially, it was really quite harmless and I enjoyed it immensely, and then he trained me for "the other."

Trained? Um, how do I have to imagine that?

That started slowly and then went on and on. For example, we once took pictures for *Beate Uhse -Shops*, first only in lingerie, then with dildos. That was great because I've always had fun with a lot of things that have to do with sex. Taking photos like that really appealed to me, and I was curious to try them out a lot more. He saw that. At some point, he asked me if I wanted to take part in the shoot. I admit that what interested me most was the room in which the models were styled. I wanted to sit in there and be made up. At some point, I said, "Okay, but only if I'm not recognized." That wasn't a problem. I could wear a wig. And then I just tried it for fun. The producer showed me everything and explained what I had to do while shooting, where I'm allowed to have my hands and where not, whether to laugh or not, and whether to look at the camera or not.

Where are you not allowed to have your hands?

Well, in front of the camera is bad; the hands must not cover anything. You also have to always look where you turn so that the camera sees everything.

What was the first pornographic film you made then?

(Laughs) Shit, how can I put this? Well, that was a gang-bang movie—with quite a lot of sperm.

That was your first movie?
Yes, that was three different recordings at once.

With how many men?
I have not counted them. I would guess between ten and fifteen, plus the audience.

Now I need a break! (I got us both a latte macchiato.) ***That's pretty cool, though, isn't it?***
I started off crass right away, yes. I am just cool! As I said, I actually wanted to work as a model for fashion and motorcycles. I even went to a professional modeling school once. And then I discovered something like that for myself. (Laughs) It was just incredibly fun for me.

Was that your first experience with group sex in the film?
No, I had my first group sex experience at the age of twenty-two, when a good friend took me to a swingers club. And that was awesome. I thought at the time: *Wow, that's like live in a porn movie!* At that time, I became curious about it and then started to consciously research further in this direction.

At your first club visit, was there immediately a gang bang?
Yes, but not myself. There was a woman who had quite a few men standing in line. That fascinated me. I asked myself, *How does she do that? That's not possible.* Back then, in my younger years, I was full of curiosity. At that time, I would never have thought that I would experience it myself.

Have you been going to clubs regularly since then?
Yes, sure, very much, but it varies on how often I go. It also depends on whether I have a partner at

the moment. Without a partner, I go more often. And if I have a partner, it depends on how he is and whether he is willing to come along. But every week is too much for me in any case.

How did that continue after this film?

I shot another gang-bang movie with the same production company a year later. During the third film, I got into a conversation with some actors who referred me to another production company that shoots private porn clips for the Internet. Through them, I came to other production companies. I also shot a fetish film with one of them. My first fetish experience was actually in the film while shooting. (Laughs)

How did you go from film to your job?

I was looking for a job, and one of the producers got me a job at the massage studio.

So, by "massage studio," I understand: I go there and get a massage.

Yes, that's what I thought too! I can massage, yes, and I did not know at first exactly what I was getting into and what was offered there. But I was curious.

Don't you say whorehouse anymore?

There are many different names for it. Each studio is different, looks different, and has different offers. I then went in there and introduced myself. After all, I've always been curious about what it looks like in there. As a woman, you don't normally get into clubs like that. I thought that was cool, and of course, it was actually quite crass again. So I spent a day looking around the studio, interviewing the female colleagues, and pestering them with questions like how they serve their customers and how it all works. Unfortunately, I wasn't allowed to watch, but all my questions were answered. I was then pragmatic: I'm looking for a job, I like to have sex, the people are very nice, so I'll just try it out.

So the men don't just come there to get massaged.

Yes, some people come just because they want a massage. However, "massage with a happy ending"—that is always part of it.

Do women actually go there?

No, they're not allowed in at all, unless they work there. Couples are theoretically possible; I would have enjoyed that. But during my time, there were never any.

What is a normal working day like?

It's really just like when you go to work in the morning. You take the train there, and on the way, you think about what you're doing. Okay, I sometimes thought: *If they knew what I was about to do.* Then you go into the club, get changed or, better, undressed, and wait for the first customers.

And they come in and pick a woman?

Yes, exactly. However, I also became active myself in terms of customer acquisition. I also had the support of the guy from the production company, who made me an internet profile, for example. I answered the letters myself, talked to the interested parties, and told them where they could find me. And then they came to me specifically. Otherwise, it's like a man comes in, into a special room where all the women introduce themselves. At that time, there were between five and twelve women. And the man chooses one.

He then goes to a room with her and stays there for an hour or how long?

It depends on what he wants to have. A quickie lasts ten to fifteen minutes and costs sixty euros. Half an hour costs one hundred euros and an hour two hundred. Most take half an hour. I get half of everything; the rest, the studio.

Also, does the stereotype of men who come in quickly for relief really exist?

Of course, there are also customers who just drop by, walk over you, and leave again. They are on a business trip or want to quickly get rid of pressure. That's the quickie for sixty euros. That's what those who have no time or no money take.

What did you learn about business on the job?

The important thing is that you stick to your times and your hourly rates. I have never sold myself short. The quickie costs sixty euros, period. I don't negotiate. And I've done a lot for my marketing and positioning, and I've looked after my customers well; I've had a lot of regular customers. It's very important that you deliver what you say you offer. That's why it was of such great importance that I come to orgasm, to a real orgasm. Because that's what the men came to me for. I showed them how it works and what to do. In addition, I have always built up a really personal connection with the guests; they have felt that I am a human being and you can also talk to me.

There is, after all, the cliché that you don't kiss. Is that still the case?

Kissing is, for some nowadays, an offer that you can buy or not. And you decide for yourself whether yes or no. I think it depends on sympathy, and I always say that on the phone. A customer once came in and asked me, "And am I likable to you?" What could I say? I didn't like him right away, and I thought: *Shit, what are you going to say now?* Those were my beginnings.

And what did you say?

Well, I then quite honestly said, "No!" and he left again. You learn over time how to kiss, what kisses you can and want to do, and what is comfortable for you. And if you don't want to kiss someone, then you just don't kiss him.

How many customers did you have during the day?

I would say about three to four; my record was ten. But then nothing worked anymore.

Isn't that incredibly exhausting, having sex all day?

Yes, it's incredibly exhausting. (Laughs) But it's also a lot of fun. Others sit in the office and sort through files or make phone calls and deal with all kinds of people. That's also exhausting. And I just had fun and got paid for it. This job gave me energy. Of course, I had good days and bad days here, too. But overall, I enjoyed it so much that I could make all the men happy.

Surely that has a lot to do with body control?

And with dedication! I learned to have an orgasm when it's his turn. You can really learn to do that.

(Laughs) How am I going to explain this? I've learned so much there, especially to surrender and give in. If you can do that, you can climax anytime, no matter with whom. That's something that happens in our bodies. My most important tip to women is to free yourself in your mind so that you can give yourself. And then you can let go in such a way that you can reach orgasm pretty quickly.

What happens physically when a man comes who you don't like at all? What do you do then? Or does it not matter?
Hmm, I would say it actually doesn't matter.

Huh?
I know this may sound strange or even absurd, but in terms of the body, it really doesn't matter. Because it's always skin, which is just sometimes firm or soft; you can either cuddle in or feel muscles. It was precisely this variety that I liked very much. The differences are mainly in the smell. That is sometimes difficult. You can have an aversion to that, which is true. But there are also solutions. If someone stinks, you put them in the shower; you're entitled to do that at any time. You can also always say no; that is also your right. But that rarely happens. Or you just close your nose and serve the customer, he's happy afterwards, and then it's also good.

But surely that doesn't work with all.
I have also turned down customers but really, very rarely. What I've learned in my job is to love everyone. I open my heart. They are all people with worries and fears. If you love everyone, you can make love to everyone. Then it doesn't matter what they look like, how tall they are, if they are fat or

thin. If you really meet someone without prejudice, open your heart and take everyone as he is, you can actually have sex with everyone. I think it's bad that many women don't treat their own partners like that.

How is it when you have so much sex professionally? Do you still enjoy it privately at all?

It makes a difference whether you do it professionally or privately. Privately, it's a completely different give and take. Professionally, you have a certain process inside and only a limited time in which you have to finish. The man wants certain things for which he pays—getting a blowjob, licking you, a massage—and it's your job to time it right. In this job, I have learned an extreme amount about leadership. I lead the man into his fun, completely letting loose myself, and all with timing. That's where you learn how to lead people and keep preset times at the same time. (Laughs) It's different in my private life, where I can enjoy myself much more, without time pressure. And it's also a difference, of course, whether with or without a condom. Professionally, there is always a barrier in between, which makes a lot of difference.

Is it different when you get money?

Yes, that too. Whether a stranger touches me for money or without money makes a big difference. I was alone in a swingers' club some time ago. That was a few weeks after I quit my job, and that's when I totally realized this: If a stranger touches me who's not my type right off the bat, I say no. I am then private and look for people who are comfortable with everything. I look differently, then. If a man pays me for a service, that's something else, a service to the man, so to speak. I give him the love for which he gives me money.

What is the biggest difference in this job compared to a "normal" job? You say you've already tried out a lot.

And that it was really fun! And I could completely determine myself. We had opening hours, which you had to stick to for the most part, but it was also possible to come later or leave earlier. I'm a mother, so if there was something wrong with my child, I could just leave. Otherwise, it was really like going to the office. You were in these rooms. There are women who are almost exclusively in the studio; they lose touch with reality. That's already a problem. It's similar to people who only sit in the office. And in the studio, of course, there's a lot of catfighting among the women, especially if you have no life and no friends outside. There are women who do this seven days a week, twenty-four hours a day. They live there and have nothing else. For me, it was more like a very well-paid hobby.

Why did you quit your job?

I met a nice man. And I wanted to get to know something new again professionally.

You must have learned a lot about men and women in this one year. What do men want during sex?

(Laughs) Squirt!

Is it really that simple?

No, not only that men want to be touched; they want to feel a woman and they want love too. I've had many men who were married and told me that

69

nothing was going on with their wives anymore, that everything had run its course. They are totally happy when they are simply embraced, caressed, and loved by a woman because they no longer got that in their relationships.

What advice can you give to women in these relationships?

Loosen up! This is the most important thing. Turn off your head, forget about the household, and observe how the man is and what does he need? The main thing is that you are in contact with the man physically. Just join in and have fun. Men like it when women have fun. And having fun is something you can learn. Many men have come to me because I always have an orgasm. That's what they wanted to experience. I have to say, though, that it wasn't like that with me before either. That only developed with this porn-shooting story. I learned to go along and surrender, even to strange men. Otherwise, you have no chance. Only through this have the orgasms arisen with me.

Should women then shoot porn movies as therapy?

Everyone has to find their own way. Letting go and loosening up in the head is the first step. The next step is to become curious about what the man does with me and where I like it. Really, feel into it first. What do I find beautiful, what do I like, and what not? If men are open, you can teach them everything. I have taught men in a very short time what they have to do to bring me to orgasm. Man must know what pleases you, then he can do exactly that. And if a man knows how to bring you to climax, then he will always go this way.

Does regular sex make you healthy?

Yes! Absolutely! What was really interesting was that the first movie producer used to say, "If people had more sex, the whole world would be a lot more peaceful." I thought that was really cool; he was right about that. That's why he produces sex films; that's his concern.

Come on.

He went to the doctor and had his blood values checked, and the doctor is always amazed that he has such incredibly good values. What he says is simple: He has sex every day. Sex makes you healthy. In the case of men, this can be measured by various values. Women evaluate it on the basis of their feeling of happiness ... and if you are happy, you are healthy!

Thank you for the insightful interview!

Chapter 8

NATURALLY BANGED

If biology had its way, we could live in harems, although nature actually invented the male only out of necessity. What can we learn from the animal kingdom, biology, and other cultures? Let's take a short excursion into nature. The transfer to our own lives can be astonishing. And this much can be revealed: It's a lot of fun!

I AM A NATURAL SCIENTIST, SO of course, I am also interested in the topic of sex from the point of view of evolutionary biology. Therefore, this chapter is quite different from the others. Sex is the most natural thing in the world, you might think. But no other animal species makes such a fuss about it as we humans do. In the animal kingdom, there's everything: monogamous, lifelong relationships that form right at first sex; harems; females that eat their males after mating; and males that ram their sperm directly into females' stomachs with a kind of spear as looking for a suitable opening would take too long. Some animals have devices on their penises to clear away the sperm of the previous male, and others find it all far too complicated, reproducing asexually. In some things, we humans differ from animals; in others, not at all. Don't worry, this is not meant to be a book about biology, but there are some very exciting things that I don't want to keep from you, dear readers. The following three things particularly struck me when I looked at nature.

As is well known, we humans have almost 99 percent of the same genetic makeup as our closest relatives, the chimpanzees. How similar are we when it comes to sex? One spring, I visited a very interesting exhibition in Stuttgart: Sex—Engine of Evolution. A whole museum just on the subject of sex, together with an accompanying book, was wonderful for my research. People had gone to the trouble of putting together everything there is to discover on this topic in nature, from the contact exchange to the first date to the day after and the question, *Why have sex at all?*

I found the section on primate sex particularly interesting because the comparison to our closest animal relatives, the apes, allows under certain circumstances conclusions to be drawn about the original human sexuality. Humans are certainly the only creatures that consciously think about sexuality (although this occasionally happens without reason). And we are the only ones who have built a very complex set of cultural, religious, and social rules around it and have almost completely disconnected this very natural instinct from the original need.

How do the chimpanzees do it? Male chimpanzees have long penises and large testicles and take just six to seven seconds to have sex! With their giant testicles, they create a veritable sperm flood in the female, and as soon as those are inside, they turn into a gel plug, similar to a large gummy bear, so that the next chimp to come along cannot successfully procreate. Chimpanzees love infidelities and not too few of them. Promiscuity is widespread among our closest relatives.

The bonobos, a species of monkey that looks very similar to chimpanzees but is much more peaceful overall, have a similar situation. In the bonobos, the women are in charge. They form groups and also have sexual contact with one another—thus, promiscuity in all directions. Bonobo males also have large testicles and fairly long penises, but they are not as aggressive as the chimpanzees. Because they prefer to resolve conflicts with sex rather than fighting, they are generally considered the hippies among primates. Interestingly, after decoding their genetic makeup, researchers have found that bonobos are more similar to humans than chimpanzees in some gene sequences.

In both monkey species, males are on average 10 to 20 percent larger and heavier than females. In the gorillas and orangutans, it is quite different. The males of these monkey species are almost twice as large and heavy as the females. They have shorter penises and smaller testicles. These monkey species live polygynously, that is, in a harem. A male has several females, which he regularly pleases. The male impresses mainly by his body size and keeps competitors away. He does not need large sex organs because he does not have to worry about one of his females cheating on him.

The gibbons are quite different: this monkey species has the smallest testicles and penises. Males and females are about the same size and weight and live monogamously. They have few fights for females, so the males need neither sprawling sex organs nor imposing body sizes.

What conclusions can be drawn about sex life from body, penis, and testicle size?

- Men in Germany are 10 to 15 centimeters taller and, on average, 20 percent heavier than women, similar to the promiscuous chimpanzees and bonobos.
- In terms of testicular size and sperm production, the promiscuous species simply need more to prevail against the many competitors. In contrast, monogamous and polygynous (i.e., harem) species have smaller testicles and fewer sperm to offer. This is not a problem if there is no

competition. Nature is thrifty. Humans are quite close to harem owners in terms of testicle size, but sperm quantity is definitely in favor of promiscuity.

- If you look at the duration and frequency of mating, you will see that the promiscuous species do it often and quickly, and the sperm are produced in no time. Here humans are more comparable to the slower harem owners and monogamous species. The duration of mating has a great influence on the bond that develops between the partners. Especially in females, the hormone oxytocin, the bonding hormone, plays a major role during orgasm. The longer the mating lasts, the stronger the bond with the partner. In humans, this rather does not speak for promiscuity.

- The females' readiness to conceive is unmistakable, especially in the promiscuous chimpanzees; their butts turn bright red as soon as they are fertile. In humans, on the other hand, it is not so obvious when the female is ovulating; this is known as hidden ovulation. A man rarely notices that his wife is fertile; most of the time, the woman herself does not notice. This fact speaks more for monogamy or harem.

- Incidentally, the human being has a comparatively large penis. This also serves, due to its special form above all, to satisfy human females better. These have comparatively large breasts in return, which serve as a sexual signal for the men.

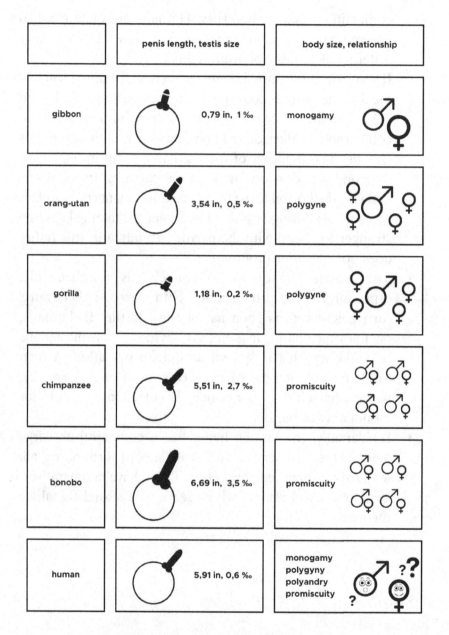

	penis length, testis size	body size, relationship
gibbon	0,79 in, 1‰	monogamy
orang-utan	3,54 in, 0,5‰	polygyne
gorilla	1,18 in, 0,2‰	polygyne
chimpanzee	5,51 in, 2,7‰	promiscuity
bonobo	6,69 in, 3,5‰	promiscuity
human	5,91 in, 0,6‰	monogamy polygyny polyandry promiscuity

What penis size has to do with polygamy

All in all, there are no clear indications from biology as to how people naturally tick sexually. We are probably too individual, and culture still plays a huge role in our lives.

Speaking of culture, ethnological records from the 1970s speak of the fact that many human societies worldwide do not live monogamously but that the preferred natural form is the harem. This, in consequence, means that many men fall by the wayside because they cannot get a woman. This is confirmed by the thesis of some molecular biologists who claim that our society today is descended from twice as many women as men. The scientists claim to have found out with the help of DNA analyses that, in the course of history, only about every third man has reproduced. In concrete terms, this means that there have always been few men who have had many children and many men who have not fathered any offspring. Interesting, isn't it?

And from the point of view of a woman, it is even understandable. All women, like strong alpha males, were very popular and were also kings, princes, knights, pirates, robbers, and bullies. Even rapists probably had better cards than the shy peasant boy next door regarding childbearing. By the way, what is relatively rare in human societies is polyandry, meaning "many-males," that is, one woman and several men. A pity, actually.

Some of what we humans do is quite different from what nature does everywhere else. Why is that? When I visited the Stuttgart sex exhibition, it struck me right at the beginning: Almost everywhere in the animal kingdom, the females are rather inconspicuous and gray and the males colorful and flashy. And the male court the favor of the females with all their biological means. Only the most beautiful, loudest, cleverest, fastest, or most daring may "get it." Men present themselves and make an effort; women choose.

With us humans, it's somehow different—at least, it seems to be in many countries, especially the civilized ones. The women are the ones who wear colorful dresses and high heels and makeup. They paint their lips red and push their breasts up with push-ups, all to please men. The men wear a uniform look with a gray suit and tie, playing it cool, and we think that's sexy. Is there something wrong? Shouldn't it be the other way around for us?

Biological fact: For women, the consequences of sex involve an infinitely higher investment than for men, and this is the case in virtually all animal species (there are very few species in which the fathers carry the children—the seahorses, for example). Carrying, nursing, and raising a child takes enormous resources, and if the wrong man is the father, he may run off and leave the woman to do it all alone. A woman can bear and raise only a limited number of children in her lifetime. Incidentally, the record is said to be sixty-nine (!) children born to a Russian woman in the eighteenth century, including twins, triplets, and I believe even sextuplets. A man can theoretically father thousands of children. But it starts much earlier. A woman brings just about five hundred eggs to maturity in her entire life, and a man produces 100 million sperm per day!

An egg cell is many times more "expensive" than sperm and is also 85,000 times larger. Oocytes are a precious commodity, and the woman has to choose very carefully whom she lets have them to avoid bad investments. She has a high risk. Men have almost no risk; instead, they have to make quite an effort to get it on with a woman. Biologically, men and women have very different goals, but they need each other to achieve them. A woman with her luxury egg instinctively takes a closer look at whom she's getting involved with. And a man with his today-cheap sperm tries everywhere; he doesn't have much to lose. So actually, everything is in the green zone. But what I wonder is, how can it be that millions of single women despair because they have the feeling that they can't get a man anymore? Is the emancipated luxury woman of today *so* demanding that she won't let any man have her? Or have men today become so unimaginative that they simply don't make an effort anymore? Have we moved so far away from our nature? And what is our nature as human beings? We are not fruit flies or bed bugs or orangutans. We have minds. We have cultures that we grew up in, and usually a religion, and those influences are enormous. The stupid thing is that Oocytes we take them so much for granted that we don't perceive them as important at all. What makes humans different from animals is that they do all kinds of cultural experiments, occasionally with negative rather than positive effects—the issue of female circumcision comes to mind. Very often, "nature is raped by culture," as evolutionary and cultural researcher Wulf Schiefenhövel put it so vividly in a lecture. What he also addresses, and what I find very exciting, is the question of whether we live culturally in a "bride-price society" or in a "dowry society"? In many cultures, an attractive young woman who agrees to marry is considered something very valuable, and the men or the men's families are willing to pay a high bride price for her. In German culture, we have the exact opposite, the dowry. There the man gets additional money if he takes a woman. Don't think that this doesn't have an influence, dear women! In very patriarchal societies, women often have little value.

I would argue that most people have absolutely no idea what a huge role culture and upbringing play in sexuality. I was born and grew up in Germany. In our culture as in every culture, certain rules are so deeply rooted that we don't even perceive them as such. In other cultures, things can be quite different. For example, it is customary in our country to no longer live with one's parents after one's midtwenties at the latest, instead living alone, in a shared apartment, or together with one's partner. It is common for parents to raise their children together and for the nuclear family to live together. And when parents separate, it's a big drama for the child, and the parents argue about which of them the child will then live with and how they will arrange it. Another example is that sex occurs in a one-night stand or an affair but preferably only in a committed relationship or marriage, and it is relatively clear what distinguishes one from the other.

Can you imagine that there are societies on this planet in which sex is completely different? Here is an example that fascinated me very much. There are still a few peoples who do not live in a patriarchal system as we do but in a matriarchy. In the patriarchal world, men are in charge; in the matriarchal world, women are in charge. What a huge difference that makes, we can hardly imagine. I recently read a book, *Paradise Is Female*, about the Musou people in Tibet, written by a journalist who lived there for a while.

These people live in a completely different context than we do. For example, there are no fathers. Of course, there are men who father children, but it doesn't matter who fathers a child because the offspring basically grow up in the mother's family. Their male role models and educators are the uncles. The Musou live in large kinship clans with matriarchs who ensure order. One child is raised by the entire extended family, and everyone takes care of everyone else. The Musou cannot imagine that it could be attractive to spend one's life with a "stranger" instead of one's own family. The idea of a nuclear family is a horror for the Musou, partly because the risk of losing everything in the event of a separation is far too high. For us, on the other hand, it is just as unimaginable: the Musou men live all their lives with their mother and her extended family in shared rooms. Only the women have their own rooms, where they receive male visitors at night. The men always come to the women, never the other way around, and women choose the men just as they feel like it. Sometimes longer "visiting visits" occur, but they can be ended at any time. A woman is free to receive the same man again and again for as long as she wants, and the man can also decide to go to the same woman again and again. It also happens, of course, that two people fall in love. Love has quite a high value even among the Musou. However, it has no consequences for the rest of their lives.

What I find particularly interesting is that both the men and the women of these people are much more relaxed and peaceful than in our culture. They don't know about wars because the men are not interested in them, and the women don't fight wars anyway. The men take care of environmental protection and agriculture. The women hold the community together and are friendly and relaxed in their dealings with one another. There is no competition among them because they do not grow up with the pressure to get the best man or even to find the "right one." They simply take the men as they are. Some theories say that, many thousands of years ago, all people were originally organized in matriarchies and worshipped goddesses because women have more wisdom in many things.

Men are the weaker sex. Why doesn't anyone know that? Why did nature invent the male? If it is only to produce offspring, we do not need sex. Sprouting also works very well, at least in plants. And asexual birth is widespread in the animal kingdom. Further, sex is exhausting and dangerous and consumes a lot of resources. So what's it all for? There is nothing in nature without a deeper meaning. And sex makes sense, or it wouldn't be the means of choice for so many species to reproduce. Ultimately, nature invented sex to create diversity. In the context of changing environmental conditions—and we have them all the time in this world—those creatures that can adapt have an advantage. Those with little different characteristics than their parents bring an advantage into the world by mixing the parental genes. By means of nonsexual reproduction, we obtain clones. Imagine that women could reproduce without men and produce clones of themselves repeatedly. In nature, this is not so rare. Many plants reproduce asexually; some animals can even do this depending on their needs. Water fleas, for example, reproduce sexually or asexually, depending on the season. In the spring, only females hatch, laying unfertilized eggs that give birth to daughters, which in turn carry unfertilized eggs in their abdomens. This is the fastest way to produce as many offspring as possible because each daughter can produce daughters again. In the fall or when environmental conditions worsen, for example, when their puddle dries up, males can also develop from the clones. Certain genes are turned on as environmental factors change, and a second sex emerges. The little animals produce eggs and sperm, and the females now carry fertilized eggs that survive periods of cold and drought. From there, the next spring, females hatch again. Flexibility sometimes makes sense.

If you look more closely, you get the impression that nature has experimented a lot with the male sex. There are more variants, more flexibility, more extravagances, and more losses. The females are always the ones who carry on life, while the males provide variation. In the animal kingdom, this is clearly visible in humans only at a second glance. For example, if you look at the heights of males and females, you will notice that most females are much closer to their average height than males. That is, the average height for men includes many very tall men and, at the same time, many very short men, whereas women tend to be similar in height. There are only a few very large or very small women, so a lot of average, but for men the average is rather rare.

The same applies to intelligence. Both the Nobel Prize and the Darwin Award (prize for the stupidest way to kill oneself) have so far been awarded almost exclusively to men. More men than women are very intelligent, but also more men are very stupid. The female sex, in turn, tends to hover around the IQ median. Men are also often more extreme in their behavior: many more boys have attention deficit disorder (ADD) and autism, and the wildest daredevils, craziest explorers, most dogged extreme athletes, and those who are the first to tread new ground—be it the highest mountains, the poles, hidden corners in the farthest rainforest, or even the moon—have always been men.

Speaking of autism, one US researcher seriously claims that autism is nothing more than an extreme form of masculinity. He's probably not completely wrong: autistic people love structures and have little to do with people and relationships; they can occupy themselves for hours with abstract things but shut down immediately when someone tries to talk to them. They usually have no empathy, can't recognize faces, and are exclusively preoccupied with themselves, but they are often highly intelligent. I think the book *Buntschatten und Fledermäuse* (*Colorful Shadows and Bats*), written by a man with autism spectrum disorder, is great. His childhood, his experiences at school, his view of the world, and especially his encounter with a girl who falls in love with him are highly interesting.

Back to men and why they are actually the weaker sex. It is common knowledge that men live shorter lives on average than women. Scientists have found out that men are weaker in their overall constitution than women from the very beginning. A male sperm with an XY chromosome is faster than the female XX sperm, but it also breaks down faster and does not last as long.

Therefore, statistically, more boys are conceived just before and just after ovulation, and girls are conceived slightly more often during sex a few days before ovulation. Miscarriages occur more often in male embryos, and girls born prematurely survive better on average than boys. Men have more strength than women, and they have a stronger drive from the start. This is due to testosterone, which is secreted in the embryo from as early as the eighth week of pregnancy. But men are also more vulnerable in some ways. My favorite brain researcher, Professor Gerald Hüther, compares masculinity in his book *Men: The Weaker Sex and Its Brain* to "an orchestra in which the timpani and trumpets have been pushed a little too far into the foreground." It is a little louder and sometimes less harmonious.

Chapter 9

GET OUT OF THE MENTAL CINEMA

Is sex just self-satisfaction on the other person's body? It's not uncommon to be in your own movie during sex, in your own thoughts, and the other person is, at best, an actor in your own mental cinema. How about exploring reality, real life? Because that is much more exciting than any movie.

Lust is energy in the body that can move.

— Pamela Behnke

T HIS CHAPTER WAS CREATED TOGETHER with Pamela Behnke, body and sex therapist and tantra massage teacher. We recorded an interview, and she wrote some texts for me, among others, about her own first experiences in tantra and in the tantra massage training. That's when I read this one sentence of hers that I got stuck on. I would never have expressed it that way myself, but when you read someone else's words, a light often comes on. It was this openly and honestly spoken sentence from her former partner: "Hey, that feels like you're masturbating with my body right now." Wow, that was a good one.

Where are you with your thoughts during sex? Are you in your mental cinema or in your body? I must admit that I know exactly what the man meant in saying that. I think most people do, but few speak it honestly. Sometimes during sex, I am almost only in my head and very little in my body, let alone with my partner. I think it is normal and simply a habit to turn on the mental cinema during sex, just as you automatically turn on the TV in the evening to relax. It also works differently, and I know that too. The way out of my head into my body was not tantra for me but consistent living out of many of my fantasies. I quickly realized that if I freed the "demons" from my head and gave them a space in my real life, they would stop haunting me uncontrollably. All of a sudden, I could enjoy intense physical sex without having to think about anything or play some mental cinema movie. I could just feel what was happening in my body. Since then, I can have sex with and without mental cinema, and I love both. To get there, there are different ways.

With tantra, I have not yet gained much experience, except for two massages from my acquaintance Chris. He was looking for a lady to practice with, and I gladly made myself available there. It was a great experience, I must say. To be pampered for over two hours and to let myself fall so completely was fantastic. I also understood at that moment that I don't need a mental cinema! It was completely sufficient to feel what he did with his hands. That was actually more exciting than anything I could ever think of! What fascinated me the most was that the yoni massaged exactly at my pace. I don't know how he did it, whether he had a particularly fine sense or whether the speed is always so slow in this massage. Or perhaps with other men, when it comes to sexual stimulation, they just can't move their hands slowly. Maybe my favorite pace is unusually slow, after all. In any case, he was the first man who had managed to manually tune into me, and he did it so well that I didn't have to add anything—neither a single thought nor the tiniest movement. This tantra massage has made me curious. I will join a course with my partner so that we can both learn it.

This experience with her partner, who uttered the all-changing sentence, was for Pamela Behnke, after years of headaches and other pains, an important sign to deal with tantra, with the art of loving consciously. And for me, it was one more reason to ask Pamela about sex. And now, I let the expert speak for herself.

Unashamed liveliness is our birthright.

Text contribution by Pamela Behnke, owner of the Zinnoberschule and head of the professional training Tantra Massage according to the criteria of the Tantra Massage Association: www.zinnoberschule.de

When I read Susanne's chapter proposals, I had to laugh heartily at how she can refreshingly name such taboo topics, and I find myself in it. How I used to feel about sex and how I feel about it today are worlds apart. I am a curious researcher in matters of love, sex, and so on. And without a doubt, I have also learned and taken a lot from the experiences with clients and participants of our tantra seminars— seminars in which many people experienced a deep connection to their own bodies, to their neighbors, and to life. Sexuality is one of the core topics that we consider valuable and important in tantra and tantra massage seminars. Sexuality is, unfortunately, still very shame- and guilt-filled. This shame and other hurts stored in the body prevent people from living aliveness fully. There is still a lot of work to be done!

Tantra Means Back to the Roots, into the Power that Creates Life!

Tantra is often associated with group sex, incense, erotic massages, or spiritual immersion in esoteric concepts, but in reality, it is about something quite different. Tantra, in its origin, is, roughly speaking, a spiritual way of harmonizing sexuality, love, and consciousness. Tantra stands for joy of living, vitality, and conscious experience. It invites us to be unashamedly alive! Tantra is an ancient deep wisdom and philosophy of life that includes a lot of respect and compassion for all aspects of life; this of course, includes the sexual nature of human beings. The tantric path was developed by Buddhist monks over two thousand years ago. There were also many developments in the Indian tradition. It has never been the purpose of life to give up your liveliness, that is, your lust for life! And what don't we do to conform to our environment and undermine our lust for life and vitality? If you give up everything else instead so that you can be alive from head to toe, in truth, you lose nothing really important, but many things will change very much, which can be scary at first. Tantra, for me, is freedom at its core: freedom from mental constructs, freedom from concepts of the mind, and freedom from structures. Tantra is a free space: it invites me and you to be as we are— alive, playful, naked. But for this, it is necessary to recognize the mental structures and concepts of the mind. You have the choice to become a plaything of your thoughts—to get on the bus, as it were, that is passing by or not, I like to say. And the beauty is this process; becoming aware of it lasts a lifetime. Tantra creates space in you for the beauty of the moment, the gift of life. That's what tantra is for me; it's liberation. And it confronts us with ourselves, and many shy away from that. It's scary to look yourself in the face so honestly, to be naked inside, to realize: *Hey, that's how I am; that's how I think if I'm honest with myself.* The gift, in my experience, is inner richness and connection to myself, to my neighbor, and to life itself.

This allows humility before life develops. Wow, I am always amazed at what happens when I am sincerely true to myself! Basically, something always happens differently than what I would have expected.

Tantrism: What Is It?

Tantrism is not a religion with dogmatic ideas but a lived philosophy that warmly invites all areas of life and breaks all constricting social structures, to bring humans as individuals into harmony with the big picture so that they can find the love and the power of the cosmos, which can experience universal unity within itself.

The word *tantra* comes from Sanskrit. Its root, *tan,* means "to expand" or "to interweave." What is meant is the great fabric of creation to which we are all connected. I, as a woman, as an individual, as a human being, as part of creation, am part of the fabric.

The whole knowledge of tantra is based on the fact that every human being is half woman and half man. In tantra, man is worshipped in his wholeness, as a part of creation, a man, a woman, a sensual-sexual being, as the initiator of life. Sexuality and ecstasy are sacred arts. Tantra unites polarities, paradoxes. Everything has two sides, and only when we can perceive both sides without bias will we begin to discover the truth. So in life, we are confronted with situations and feelings that are beautiful or unpleasant, we evaluate something as good or bad, but each side wants to be felt and accepted so that we can say yes to ourselves. Then a transformation happens: what is, maybe, and what is allowed to be can change.

Tantra massage is not a protected concept, which often leads to misconceptions. And the tantra massage is not the same as tantra! Tantra massages are often offered for a lot of money, with the main goal of achieving an orgasm or ejaculation. But that is not the point. However, that does not mean that orgasms or ejaculations are taboo! There are different philosophies about this. Tantra massage is an aspect of bodily awareness in the tantric school of life and love. In addition, the person may experience the beauty and dignity of the "temple body." I appreciate this kind of temple service to the body of God incredibly, if I may put it poetically. For me, the key to the tantric massage ritual is relaxation in the present moment. To be caressed, touched, and massaged in a secure setting. Firm and light touches alternate; sensual impressions for eyes, ears, nose, and mouth are part of the worship ritual along with well-founded massage techniques. Every part of the body gets the same attention, including the sensitive intimate area, which usually gets attention only when it comes to pursuing a specific goal. Just in the aimless turning to our sensitive areas lies a great wealth of emotions, pent-up energy can become available for the whole organism. The pleasure potential—the pleasure in life and feeling—becomes more colorful, more lively. I know tantra massage is, unfortunately, often associated with sexual services. I definitely have other experiences with it in ally seminars! I accompany people to truly feel themselves. Many grateful participants confirm afterwards that they have never felt like this in their entire lives. Sad, but true.

For Men Only: Lingam Massage

Orgasm is not equal to ejaculation, through surrender to male power! Lingam massage is a departure into a new male sexual experience. It is about relaxation and surrender, about letting things

89

happen, receiving them instead of expecting them, and actively doing something.

It is a great challenge for men to experience receiving a deeper perception of their own sexual potency or life force and an increase in sexual fulfillment. The pleasurable and perhaps challenging part of the massage is to recognize the one-way street thinking (touch + arousal + orgasm = ejaculation) as such and to open oneself to new experiences in favor of a constantly increasing abundance of orgasmic energy throughout the body. This means that, by not ejaculating every time, the sexual energy can spread to the whole body. It is a fantastic experience. It might not be much fun at the beginning to do without the usual ejaculation; otherwise, the built-up sexual tension is discharged until the moment when the goal of the touch dissolves in surrender to the here and now. One experiences an orgasmic feeling throughout the body. The gift is great and not just in the realm of sexual pleasure. People who experience this feel differently about themselves and about life, even in everyday life. The lust for life expands. I find this a very interesting introspection: how much lust can I hold, or endure, before I have to get rid of it again, before I reach a turning point? From my own giving and accompanying participation, I can say that, through the lingam massage, which is embedded in an extensive tantra massage worship ritual, men always experience something new about themselves; they explore, enjoy, give themselves into their lust, and feel a whole new power of sexual energy.

Do you dream of being a good lover? Would you like to learn which skills will take you further? When we go into the body with our attention, we know from the gut out what is coherent at the moment. Sex is, first and foremost, a physical thing, not a thing of the mind. The deeper the ecstasy, the deeper the experience of oneness and unity; the deeper the bodily experience, the more ingenious the mind automatically becomes. One is related to the other but not in the way most think.

Heart and Lust

I admit that this is easier said than done. Every day I meet men and women in my practice for psychotherapy and sex therapy who, despite the apparent enlightenment of our society in matters of sex and the like, are far from fulfilled sexuality. Sure, people are screwing, and the market offers all kinds of game variations, but when I hear how people are doing, I sometimes ask myself, *What's the point of the circus?* For a mediocre orgasm. Discharge of sexual excitement. Tantra offers us a concrete and practical way to experience deeper fulfillment and lust for life. And that starts with being aware of our own needs and feelings.

When I came to tantra in my early twenties, I had just finished my training as a yoga teacher, was in a relationship, already had a daughter, and also liked sex. I didn't know there was so incredibly much more to it, so I didn't miss anything either. The measure of things was the hunt for orgasm and what to do to get it. Fair enough, but far from fulfilling. I was satisfied. But being fulfilled in sexuality and life is different from getting off on or with someone else. As my partner said once o beautifully and honestly at that time, that for him our sex felt like I was masturbating with his body, I became thoughtful. He was right, only I had no alternative at all. I knew what he meant but knew nothing else. What else? Nothing against head cinema, nothing against masturbation on the other—the question is whether I have a choice or not.

There was nothing more than the trail of excitement, which I was hanging onto like a thread.

Since my partner at the time was a very lustful man, I gave him a tantra massage on a whim and thought to myself afterwards, *Man, why do I give away something like that only to others and not give it to myself?* I then signed up for a basic training tantra massage; I was always curious. And I thought to myself that I would certainly learn how to touch my partner more wonderfully. I never thought that I would learn something about myself. So the fact that I was actually full of shame and far away from a loving relationship with myself and my body shook me up quite a bit when I stood naked in the massage class for the first time. Seven days of giving and receiving appreciation, adoration, and sensual loving touch that, after a short time, blew my inner walls of physical tension. There was no more restraint possible and necessary. I just cried with touch. To feel how I was finely and subtly tuned like an instrument, to experience the quiet tones of sensual feeling, the sensitization of one's own perception for how arousal moves in the body and spreads to the heart. In tantra, we speak of the connection between sex and the heart. To connect the desire with love, to inhabit both poles.

The tantra massage ritual has also made it clear to me in only a short time that what I knew as an orgasm until now is actually only a short discharge of a few seconds, comparable to a hiccup, just the tip of the iceberg. I have learned: There is more! And for this, not even the genital touch is necessary. There is a lot of ignorance about lust and love and, ultimately, about the lust for life and the love of life. In tantra, we can rediscover this knowledge.

Find Access to Your Own Body: Love Yourself First!

Sexuality has a lot to do with feeling yourself in your body. Can you feel yourself, just like that, without actually touching yourself? Try it once, wherever you are sitting or standing. The good things are simple! Wander with your attention from top to bottom through your body; take your time. Do you feel the areas of your body? Are there areas that you are not aware of? In seminars or sex counseling, I often hear after such a body experience, "Gee, that's a thing!" I always thought I could feel myself, but when I take my time, I realize I'm way off, not to mention my vagina or penis and pelvic floor. If you don't feel yourself, you are not at home with yourself. The breath helps you to engage in the present sensing of your body. So take a few conscious breaths and join your breath as it moves in and out of your body right now, as you read. You don't need to change your breath; you don't need to control it. How is your breath flowing? Is it shallow and felt in the chest? Does it flow deep into the belly? Can you feel it moving your body as you inhale and exhale? Why is this relevant? If you breathe more, you feel more. Everyone probably knows that you breathe more shallowly or stop breathing in a stressful or scary situation. If you want to try something new, do something different, breathe in that situation. Then something will change. Let yourself be surprised. The feeling changes—you can get out of old patterns simply by changing your breath. This also works during sex: The more and more consciously you breathe, the greater the energy! This can also be loud and strong. The importance of the breath has unfortunately been forgotten in our culture with its taboo attitude towards sex.

Exercise: Bodyscan

Stand comfortably with soft knees. Wander with your attention through your body. Where do you feel yourself?

Now put on a groovy piece of music, move to it and shake your entire body to the music. After that, stand comfortably again and notice your body now.

Is there a difference? Do you feel yourself more clearly? What does that mean in concrete terms? What do you feel more clearly? And how does the difference feel? Tingling ants, pulsating somewhere? Do you feel your heart beating now? The expansion through your breath? If your body may twitch, then allow it, then tension is discharged; wonderful. That's how simple it is. If the body is not awake, the head cinema takes over. The next time you have sex, go slowly and feel if you perceive the penis inside you. If you are a man, feel if you can feel the vagina surrounding you. A great exercise for women: Leave one or two fingers in your vagina and move them consciously. Do you feel it internally if you are touching on the top or bottom or left or right, if the cervix is being touched or if the finger is resting still? Don't leave it to someone else; your body and your sex belong in your own hands! This will increase your self-confidence and your trust in yourself.

Yin-yang: The Tantric Royal Game of Love

With the royal game, you can always have new experiences in the field of partnership and sexuality, even if it is not superficially about sex at first. If you have desire, an exploratory spirit, and curiosity about yourself and your partner, then the king game is just right for you! Even if you have known each other for years, it opens up new dimensions or encounters of trust, engagement, and intimacy.

From my own experience, I can say that it is a beautiful way to spend the morning or the whole day together and create closeness, especially when you are not so close or just dead pants. Decide at the beginning who is going to be king first and who wants to be involved in the devotion of service. And the time frame—two, four, or six hours? I recommend the extensive option. Then at a later time or on another day, there is the role reversal. The "kings" calmly share their needs and desires, and the "servants" can decide whether they want to give themselves wholeheartedly to the desire and decide which desires to fulfill and which not. You, as the king, can notice if you are getting out of your own way and denying desires and needs. Expressing yourself, showing yourself—that alone is worth a lot. Remember, no wish has to be fulfilled; those who serve have the freedom to do only that which they put their hearts into.

As a servant, you may need to take a deep breath. Perhaps a wish is expressed that demands a lot of you. Push your comfort limit! Wonderful! Then you realize that you have a limit and where it lies. Decide to try it out, or suggest a variation if it doesn't work at all. You carry the responsibility for yourself! My experience has shown that many desires and needs first follow a pattern. The exciting thing happens after they have been fulfilled. If you then, as a king, only feel out of the moment regarding what you want now, it can be that you feel nothing at all and are uncertain. Right behind it, if you take your time, new things can emerge from the moment and contact with your partner.

Orgasms? About the Hunt for Orgasms

In tantra, we speak of peak or valley orgasms. Peak orgasms are familiar to many people. The excitement builds and discharges at the point of greatest tension and charge, like a dolphin leaping out of the water, the water splashing, the yang. Valley orgasms are wide and expanding in quality of sensation, sweet and soft, like a whale surfacing and gliding back into the water, the yin.

Most of us suspect happiness behind every next corner and "have to have orgasms." The source of these orgasms is the brain: we feel impulses from the mind or inner images, less from the body! The search for the kick, the sexual excitement and discharge drives many. Only it is often hard work to achieve an orgasm. Have you ever observed what the path to orgasm looks like? Playful or real work to climb to the top, or maybe even uncomfortable or impossible for you? Really, many women have a problem experiencing orgasm and wonder what's wrong with them. Many men deal with the fact that they ejaculate too soon or "can't." When we start to let go, relax, notice our needs and make them important, and take the focus away from the orgasm goal, the energy in the body can build. When we stop working hard, the energy is held in our system. The body is like a clinical thermometer; in a narrow space, the temperature and energy rise differently than in a wide vessel.

Orgasm and Ecstasy

Every person has an inner magnetism, a positive and a negative pole. This is the source of our higher orgasmic experiences.

Know how! Breath, body tension, movement, and voice are central keys to consciously direct the inner operating temperature.

Orgasm is not a matter of luck! Basically, human beings are like magnets, just as our planet has a magnetic field, the north and south poles. One pole is in the chest, and one is in the genitals.

What happens in between? A flow of energy. And that's where it gets interesting. Men and women are different. Equal forces but opposite, which complement each other ingeniously. What happens between magnets that meet at opposite ends? They attract each other. Then energy flows. This energy can flow in a circuit, within ourselves and between ourselves and our partners, even without hard work! However, many of us have unlearned this ability. That is, there is always tension in us; we find it hard to believe that there is a whole different way to have sex, a way that can be much more fulfilling and touching! We experience it when we change the habit of chasing orgasm and having hot sex. What happens: We become more magnetic, and the attraction of men and women to each other grows. There is energy moving between man and woman. This is possibly a new image of sex. The result: we can become more balanced and loving in our everyday interactions. Such an ingenious, natural thing, and we don't know it anymore! And we work hard to find ecstasy, while it is basically already there without any doing, but we don't know how to do it. So how can you have this other, energetic sex?

Activating the inner magnet means experiencing a new form of sex! The positive pole of women is in the breasts and heart. Energy is generated in the positive pole, and women give and nurture from that positive pole. The positive pole is ready. In men, the positive pole is in the genitals, the penis, the perineum, and the grundle. The negative, receptive pole is the heart in the man and the genitals in the woman. Energy flows from the positive pole to the negative, both within the earth and within man, and from man to woman and woman to man.

We all know what happens when sexual energy is suppressed in women. When the receptive pole of women is not "used" and cannot open up, they eventually lose interest in sex. This is not necessarily psychological; it does not mean frigidity. It is that the body that no longer likes to open and no longer feels like it. Why? Because the woman is not really female alive. She can be aroused, let the man in, and at the same time not really be open. Have you ever noticed that you can physically feel really open with every fiber of your body to receive your partner? Since the woman's breast is the positive pole, that is, the source of sexual energy, it is very important that the energy flows from the breasts to the genitals. Only in this way can the woman open up from the inside. If you have breastfed a child, you may know the connection between breast and genitalia; breastfeeding pulls up into the uterus. There this connection is very clearly felt, only women often do not even allow themselves this pleasurable feeling. It's like an open secret! Often one concentrates only on the partner, but not on activating the inner magnet of oneself first. In order to appreciate sex over a longer period of time, the woman must realize that her source of sexual energy is in the breasts. Thus, the breast is initially more important than the pelvis. I think many women don't know this at all. Diana Richardson, a tantra teacher I value, encourages women in her lectures: Love your breasts, wake them up! No, not stimulate them, wake them up! This supports women to become more confident in their femininity. There is a lot of fear among women because they think there is something wrong with them, the breasts are too small or too big or whatever. No, nothing is wrong. Everything is fine the way it is! When women get the time to open up, they love sex.

To the men, Diana Richardson encourages, Go with your consciousness into your positive pole all the way down into the pelvis, into the perineum, just as women go into the breasts and nipples. Connect your positive pole to your receptive pole, your heart. The energy in your inner circuit is a kind of inner marriage of lust and love, pelvis and heart, and getting this energy flowing with the help of your attention and breath is important to activate your magnet! Do you have a strong urge for something great to happen as quickly as possible? Then you are in the head. Maybe it's about you first relaxing during sex, noticing tension, and allowing feelings.

That is already enough so that the energy in you can begin to flow.

And remember: If you want to feel, you have to breathe!

Sex with Yourself: Connect Your Poles with Each Other

Connect in your imagination your positive, giving pole with your negative, receptive pole. You can imagine light flowing between these two poles or your breath or whatever is right for you. Make the connection and let the energy flow. And rest with it in yourself. Feel the two poles in your body from the inside out. Realize that you are a magnet inside. The energy in your inner circuit is like inner sex. Whether you have a partner or not, you can always let this energy flow within you, which is very nourishing for body, mind, and soul. It can take a long time to feel this inner connection, but it is really worth it! Do you think this is boring? Provocatively, I would say noticing boredom is an important thing.

You notice with which inner attitude and with which inner sympathy you are at the moment. Boredom is a thought from a nonsensical attitude. As long as you think about it, you will not feel it.

Ecstasy is the oneness with the body, to be totally absorbed in it and in being in the moment without striving or wanting anything. Freedom of purpose. Trust your body! Getting from insensitivity to sensitivity takes time. Take it; it is worth it! We are not really in our bodies and look at the body from the outside and think, *Hey, why don't you do what I want you to do?* Function the hell out of it! There is so much more we can live as humans that no one has taught us. Experience shows that connecting more with our bodies remarkably impacts health and quality of life. And the beautiful side effect of being more present in our own body is that the energy between the pelvis and the heart begins to flow and the heart opens.

Sex Is a Celebration. Celebrate It!

Below are some small experiments that will help you to reconnect with your body. Have fun with it!

Experiment 1: Ecstasy and Attention

Wherever you are sitting or standing, look around and look for something green. Where can you find something that is green? Take a few minutes to do this. You will probably find that when you fixate on green, you block out the rest automatically. It's the same with the search for ecstasy. If you're on the track to finding just that, you're missing out on what's actually ecstatic!

Experiment 2: With a Lot of Rubbing Is Now Over!

Rub your left forearm quickly with your right hand for two minutes.

How did it feel?

Now slowly rub your left forearm with your right hand for two minutes, varying speed and pressure.

How did that feel? How was your breathing?

Now slowly rub your left forearm with your right hand for two minutes, touching yourself so that it feels nice.

Where was your attention this time? How was your breath? Your body tension?

Experiment 3: Fantasy and Reality

What fantasies do you have? What is the need behind your fantasy? I would say very radically that people who don't know fulfillment in their own bodies is more likely to resort to fantasy than those who can surrender themselves and savor every moment. If reality is fulfilling, why be in your head instead?

Find out what your true need is. Allow yourself this thought, and form it concretely. How does it look? Which sounds belong to it? How does it smell? Which people are present? Be there with all your senses. And when the moral club comes from the depths of your mind, take a deep breath.

Experiment 4: Move and Let Your Voice Sound

When experiencing intense, physical joy, what could be more natural than moving, squealing, and screaming? We are among the living beings who can express ourselves with our bodies. How unnatural it is not to move, squirm, wrestle, or fight with each other during sex—just like not breathing, singing, moaning, or sighing! Let your sex be alive, visible and audible. Sex is a gift! What do people do when they celebrate? They dance and sing. Therefore, celebrate when you have sex.

Group Sex with Incense Sticks?

About tantra, spirituality, and people exploring their lust together

Interview with Pamela Behnke, expert in tantra and tantra massages, lecturer for sexual and psychotherapy. Owner of Zinnober, competence center for sexual education: www.zinnoberschule.de.

Pamela, thanks for the great text and suggestions. I now have a few more questions that are bothering me. You wrote above that tantra was developed by monks. How does that fit together?

Sexual energy is one of the strongest energies there is. It is, after all, the source of life. The monks knew it very well and knew how to handle and use this energy. They included it and did not exclude it. Unfortunately, in many spiritual and religious schools, sexuality is not addressed; even in most yoga schools, sex does not get any space. For me, it is clear: sexuality is life, and true spirituality can only arise if one also uses this energy.

I once heard that in tantra courses, there are many voyeurs and exhibitionists. Is that true?

I find this question amazing because I haven't thought about this before. Officially, it is certainly not so. I know that the topics of showing oneself consciously or looking consciously are valuable and important for many people. Last but not least, it is about the topic of self-worth and respectful sympathy.

In the group, you are completely naked at some point, which is certainly a situation that not everyone wants to expose themselves to. But maybe that's exactly what some are looking for there?

The responsibility of whether or not to undress is up to each person. It is of great concern to us that everyone feels and perceives their own limits and needs and acts accordingly. Certainly, there are many people who are curious about such an experience. And that is perfectly okay. But the participants experience in the course that it is about something else, namely, feeling themselves and opening the heart. In the process, you quickly realize: I can stand there quite naked, even if I'm still dressed! One also feels naked spiritually and it is secure. The course is about a sincere encounter with another person, an encounter from heart to heart, and about the connection between lust and love. People have to bring the willingness to deal with these things; otherwise, the seminar is not the right one. I have tried out, learned a lot, and got involved in many "extreme" things. There was even a seminar where the toilet doors were unhooked. Nothing was hidden or denied anymore. But that's not always the case, don't worry.

What was your most moving experience during your training?

I took part in an annual program where we were supposed to perform a certain ritual, and I was the only one left who no one wanted to do it with. That was very bad for me at first. I asked myself, *What is wrong with me?* But it had nothing to do with me but with my practice partner, who couldn't get involved. I decided to join anyway, sat down on a pile of mats between all these men and women in this beautifully decorated room, and felt like Buddha. I had to cry snot and water. It was so touching and brilliant to watch. So many people being mindful and loving with each other, and so intimate to boot; for me, it was like a deep longing. When does one have such an opportunity? The pure horniness can certainly be observed in a swingers club, and the love level can be experienced in any tearjerker novel. But both together.

But they didn't have sex there?

No, it was not about sex but about the issues involved. Touch, trust, surrender. The question is, Where does sex begin? In this ritual, people did not have sexual intercourse. It was a worship ritual with yoni and lingam massages. I actually already knew this, but at this moment, it was something very special again.

In tantra, there is often talk of ecstasy. What exactly is meant by this?

Ecstasy in tantra is something cool, nothing hot or horny. Because consciousness comes into it, after all, it's about the two primordial forces, Shiva and Shakti. Shakti is the pole of sexual power, and Shiva is consciousness. And when the two come together, then something cool is created, not "hot stuff." Cool in the sense of clear. By that, I don't mean control, but real wakefulness, consciousness. This is in no way boring. You are in the highest excitement and, at the same time, awake, and you get every single feeling much more consciously. Then you are not out of your senses, quite the opposite, but with all your senses. That is real sensuality.

How did you get the idea to start a love school?

That wasn't a conscious decision at the beginning. There was actually something else on my life plan. In my early twenties, I wanted to become a midwife. Well, actually, I'm a midwife now, too, on a different level. I was pregnant and took a yoga teacher training course. Yoga was very good for me at that time. From yoga to tantra was just a small step, and then I realized that it does me even better! I also had health problems at that time, often headaches, and I didn't know why.

And the headaches have gone away with the help of tantra?

Yes, and overall I got so much more strength and desire for life. That was insane, a real milestone in my life! I really got into a flow; that was exactly my thing. Because I felt and released so much on the inside, the doors also opened on the outside. Many things that I used to have to work hard for suddenly happened on their own. Surrendering, trusting, and tolerance—that's what it's all about. It was a blessing for me that I discovered this so early on. Desire and lust for life; that's very closely related.

You could say that you have turned your hobby into a profession!

Yes! I realized then that I wanted to fill my life with what does me the best. That was never part of the plan and has developed bit by bit and continues to grow. It's important to keep connecting with that vision, and that's what my work asks me to do. I think many people, even if they experience it once, lose it again. You have to keep at it! I love to feel myself, and the feedback from the participants is that they can feel me too.

What kind of people come to you, and what do they want to learn from you?

Above all, people come who want to find access to their sexuality again ask themselves the question: "Should that be all there is in life?" Some come because they are exhausted and resigned and do not know how to experience a fulfilling sexuality. And others are simply curious. Every person is different, has a different motivation and their own needs, and sexuality.

Do tantra and SM fit together?

Lately, I've been consciously trying out what it's like to tighten my grip during sex. And I've noticed that it sharpens the presence. It's about being very awake, always looking at what I feel, what the other person feels, is it still right? That is a very conscious process. It is also about the question: Why are you doing this? What is your motivation? If you are clear about this, it can be very enriching.

But sex therapy and tantric massage do not go together.

At least not in Catholic Bavaria! There you have to register as a prostitute if you want to perform Tantra massages. Only doctors and midwives are allowed to touch genitals; alternative practitioners are not allowed. However, one should also know that tantra massages are often offered where they actually do not belong. These are then "deceptive packages," where it is actually about prostitution. A real tantric massage is something different. It is about deep touch and appreciation.

When did you start researching the field of sexuality?

For me, the interest started very early. At the beginning, it was pure childlike curiosity, just like children want to try out and get to know everything, including their own bodies. I was lucky—my parents were very open about it, and I experienced the typical childhood doctor games without anything being problematic about it. This normal child development is disturbed in many adolescents because their parents give them the feeling that something is wrong. You can't compare child sexuality with adult sexuality. With children, it's completely uninhibited, simply curious, interested, and not goal-oriented. For me, it was clear that my parents were sexually active; sometimes, I heard them, and that was completely okay and natural. For many people, that is the horror par excellence: their own parents having sex with each other. Because sexuality was not hidden from me, I was also able to deal with this topic very naturally. I had my first experience with boys at the age of thirteen, and by then, I knew myself very well. I simply tried out a lot, quite playfully. When I was fourteen, I once stuck a dildo up my boyfriend's butt simply because I wanted to know what it was like, completely at ease. At that time, I didn't even know that one could be ashamed of something like that.

But then there was also once a phase of shame and self-consciousness.

I had a new partner, and with him, I was suddenly ashamed of everything. He was not that easy, and then suddenly, I wasn't either. With him, I couldn't talk during sex, and my play instinct was gone. He was a few years older. Not talking was, I think, the crucial point. To exchange, what does me good, what does you good—that was completely missing. His reluctance became mine. I sensed that somehow, but I couldn't address that either.

How did you rediscover your play instinct?

It was with another partner who very much appreciated my openness. For him, it was very beneficial. He enjoyed it. He then also became the father of my son.

What turns you on the most?

It depends on the mood, and it varies a lot. I very much appreciate silent sex. Not always. I also like it very dynamic and archaic. But not always, either. It depends on how the moment is. Life changes all the time. I'm variable there. In me, there are these two sides and many more shades in between.

What do you mean by "silent sex"?

Do not move or move very slowly. What always impresses me very much is to feel how the genitals then communicate with each other. The energy flows without me having to actively do anything. Neither friction nor pressure, nor any other "action." A dialogue develops between the genitals and bodies. And an incredible depth.

You also recommend this to women who do not have orgasms.

Yes. Many women are stuck in a vicious circle: they have no connection to their genital organs and can hardly feel themselves; their intravaginal tissue is as if armored internally. They then think they need more and more to feel anything, and the man has to work harder and harder for them to feel anything at all. But this dulls them more and more. It is actually a very good exercise to then consciously move very slowly and very little for once. Being in each other's presence and just feeling once. It is important to look into each other's eyes. Connect with the heart. This creates a dimension of depth in the mind, and usually a whole new feeling in the body. When I work with women in the field of tantra massages, I involve the whole body; the woman is invited to move the pelvis and also the chest very slowly. It's like a wave movement through the whole body. My experience: connecting with your partner in a genitally mindful way also brings peace and mindfulness to everyday life, to a couple's relationship. Those who have sex in this way argue differently.

Let me ask you a very practical question: If I want to try this out, how much time should I set aside for it?

That's a good question. How long does sex last? Of course, time is a decisive factor. The question is, how important is it to you?

If it is important to you, then, of course, you take more time. If this gives you strength and you want to deepen your relationship with your partner, then you should take the time that is necessary for this and also not look at the clock.

It's also important to know that if you're just waiting for, "When is ecstasy going to come?" and you're expecting something very specific, it's like being in a room and looking around and just looking for something green. I described that in an exercise above. You might find a green, but you don't notice anything else. It is similar to silent sex. Stay alert and feel everything that happens.

And you find something green, something brown, something black, something yellow. It's about noticing all of that, all of the hues, all of the in-betweens. To be alert, mindful, and attentive, to arrive in the here and now.

Does it make sense to do it with soft music?

I would try it out. The music should not distract you. It is important that you first come to yourself, feel yourself and realize what kind of film is running in your head. Then you realize at some point ... *aah* ... *hmm*! I have to grin right away.

Did you experience an orgasm in your training that was completely different from everything before?

Orgasm is actually something different than I thought, and it has nothing to do with genitals. I experienced it in my first tantra class. A truly orgasmic state that was triggered solely by a touch on my hand. That was a huge realization for me, and I thought, *If this is already going on, where is this going to lead?* Then probably many things are quite different than I actually thought. That made me really curious.

Orgasm has nothing to do with genitals?

An orgasm is a state of surrender, of opening up; you let the energy flow. This can go through the whole body and possibly be triggered by a small touch anywhere on the body. However, it takes a lot: deep surrender and relaxation. Letting go and stop trying to be a good lover or look perfect. Sometimes tears have to flow first.

Can I have a great orgasm if I stop being a good lover? It's best to stop wanting to be anyone at all. Most of the time, during sex, one's attention is more focused on the other person than on oneself, trying somehow to please the other person. When both do that, no one is at home. A good exercise is to take turns pampering each other, one giving and one taking. And the one taking concentrates only on himself on what the body feels, what it likes, what it doesn't. This is a great experience for both.

What else are you curious about yourself?

On everything! (Laughs) Of course, some tantric practices I have yet or not done consistently. For example, you can use the sexual energy of orgasm to bring into life a new thought, a vision or to create something new in your life, like planting a seed in fertile soil. The high energy that is there at that moment can be compared to very strong motivation. It can move mountains. It is very common in tantra to use orgasmic energy and not just let it fizzle out. What I also always find exciting is a sexual encounter with my partner, where I don't know at all beforehand what will happen.

Isn't it always the case that you don't know what's going to happen beforehand?

Sure, in the best case, yes. But for many people, it's like this: Oh yes, I already know him; we've had sex a hundred times. And it always follows a similar pattern. You already know at the beginning how it will end. It's enough to consciously ask yourself once, *What do I think it will be like today? What do I really want? What is my partner in the mood for?* Maybe it will be quiet sex; maybe it will be rather intense; maybe it will be completely different. And let yourself get involved with everything that arises without images in your head.

You deal with sexuality every day in your job. What does a sex therapist do for her own sex life?

I have definitely resolved to take more time again for the feminine aspect of my life, relaxation, and devotion. In the last few years, I've been on the road a lot in business matters and very much in my masculine power. So it is important not to neglect the other part. To reconnect with my pelvis and my female organs, I relax and let go. That grounds me, brings me down. Specifically, I should enjoy extensive and many yoni massages!

Thank you very much for the exciting interview!

Chapter 10

LONGING FOR DEVOTION

Experience the pleasure of losing control. When you live who you are and say what you want, sex is a new adventure every time. Your relationships change. Sex doesn't get worse with time, it gets better!

> O tempora, o mores! (What are these times, what are these mores!)
>
> — Cicero

BEFORE WE RETURN TO MY own story after the excursions into nature and tantra, here is a brief digression into the ancient Greeks. Greek mythology tells the story of Pandora, who brought people a box containing all the vices in the world. Because people were so curious and opened the box despite the prohibition, we have much evil in the world today. Once opened, more and more evil came out of that box, and there was no stopping it. Actually, it's a silly story. I would like to rewrite it! How would it be if not Pandora, but Aphrodite, the goddess of love, beauty, and sensuality, had brought a box to the people that contained a lot of fun and love? How would it be if *that* were spread inexorably after opening? Because actually, lust for life works according to this principle.

Once you have discovered it for yourself and curiously "opened" it, it multiplies! That is my experience, and life confirms it to me again and again. Every day anew. Good things multiply—and not only when it comes to sex.

But let's stay on the subject of sex for once; after all, that's what this book is about. You might ask me if SM preferences, fetishes, sex clubs, and parties become routine and boring at some point, just like "normal sex" often does. What I believe is that, for whatever game you choose, if it is really yours and gives you fulfillment, you will *never* be bored. Because if you are curious about something, you will have a new experience every time. At this point, I would like to again quote a Greek, namely Heraclitus. He said five hundred years before Christ, "You can never get into the same river twice. The water is different, and the person is different."

He also said, "Panta rhei," meaning, "Everything flows." If you are curious about sex, you will dive deeper and deeper into the physical-spiritual-emotional dimension and constantly experience new aspects of yourself, your partner, and the interaction of the two bodies. You will constantly have new experiences and always experience different orgasms.

Whoever has found "his thing," his kind of sex, will never be bored with sex again! Life itself is not boring. Think back to your childhood. Christmas and birthdays were exciting every time. As a child, you looked forward to everything. Everything was exciting, even if you went to the same toy store for the hundredth time. If you turn your passion into a career, you'll never complain about being bored at work again. And if you discover your favorite sex, you'll always enjoy it.

This has only to do with ourselves, less with our environment or our fellow human beings. It's down to our level of curiosity and our ability to feel joy. Thinking back, I could rave and be enthused about every single night in a club or at a party because each one was completely unique, and each would be worth writing about. I wondered for quite some time how the parties could have gotten better each time. I always thought, *This party today is even better than the last one,* and *Wow, this is the coolest night I've ever had!* I realized at some point that I feel this way because I open up more and more, live out, self-realize, and increasingly live who I am and what I really want because I always perceive more and carry growing joy within myself. For someone who has little to gain from these experiences in the area of sex, parties are perhaps boring at some point. For me, it is a highlight every time and always as exciting as the first time.

When does it feel like the first time for you? When in your life do *you* experience that feeling of excitement, of butterflies in your stomach? What is your favorite sex? How can we recognize really good sex? There is an unmistakable sign that people have found their favorite sex. At least from the outside, you can observe it very well. They starts to glow. The eyes light up, the skin becomes brighter, and you can literally feel their positive energy. They bubble over with the joy of living and fun, radiating attractiveness! You can see the difference from before to after. Whether they are then exhausted or wide awake, they are more beautiful, more attractive than before.

What makes you and your partner shine? What "turns on the lights" for both of you? I once consciously observed exactly that at the parties because people like I've just described are there, too. They light up the whole evening like a firework. I am such a person, and I know several others. You can tell when a person is satisfied, happy, and peaceful. And there are others who look just as pale and uninspired as when they walked in, even after a two-hour SM session. You get the feeling that they just worked through some program. Sure, there are good and bad days for everyone, you could say. But if you do your thing, what really fulfills you, every bad day immediately becomes a good day. Can you feel for yourself what really makes you good and makes you shine? If you honestly feel it, yes. But I believe that most people either can't feel it accurately or don't allow the truth at all because morals, reason, and who knows what else are stronger. Even at SM parties, you can remain uninspired in the truest sense of the word. It takes more to become truly free.

I had my absolute sexual highlight in the summer of 2010, five years after I started my research journey. That summer, I met a man who was my exact counterpart sexually. He loved in exactly the same way as me, only in the other role. I was passive, and he was active. Interestingly, in order for that to be possible, something else in my life had to die, and that hurt me a lot. Because, in this case, it was a relationship with someone I had loved very much and who left me virtually overnight. We had a very deep and genuine heart connection, we were going to move in together and start a family, but at some point, he got cold feet and was gone. Ouch. I guess I was too extreme for him after all.

During this time, I was back in the SM scene more often and went to the regulars' table meetings, and it was on one of these evenings when I met him, "Mr. Magic." He was there with his wife, and we immediately connected. He was eloquent, educated, and funny, and we laughed a lot. It was soon clear that we wanted to play together. An affair with a married man had always been taboo for me; I didn't want to be a second wife. Surprisingly, I didn't care about him, my heart was broken anyway, and this would become a pure-play relationship, just like going to the movies or sporting events with friends. I was no competition at all for his wife. This was all about one thing: discovering a very specific kind of pleasure together. He knew very well about the active role, and even our first meeting was a blast. It was lunchtime, and he came with his toy bag, like Paul had done in the past. I knew I could trust him. There was no safe word, no arrangement beforehand—that wasn't necessary at all.

The first thing he did, even before he took off his jacket, was to put metal hand and foot cuffs on me. It went through me like a lightning bolt. Is it a pleasant feeling when someone else takes control? I couldn't help but surrender and let go, relax. There was nothing to do but be horny. All the clocks stopped. We sat on the balcony and chatted a bit. It was a bizarre situation. *I hope no one sees me here,* I thought. I felt arousal spreading through my body, and I couldn't do anything about it. I felt aroused and secure at the same time; it's hard to describe. There are no words for it. Many types of arousal exist, and one word can't capture the subtle

113

differences, just as the Eskimos can name many kinds of snow while we can barely distinguish between "wet snow" and "powdery snow."

Even as I laboriously moved to the kitchen to make us a coffee, the excitement remained. The restriction in movement immediately awakened mindfulness. I carefully took one small step after the other. Mr. Magic followed me into the kitchen; he had something else planned for me before the coffee break. He slowly led me down the stairs to the basement and opened the handcuffs, only to close them again immediately behind my back. Again, this lightning flashed through me. The excitement inevitably increased. He placed me under the stairs, wrapped a rope around the banister and my hands at the same time, and slowly pulled my arms up behind my back. I had to bend my upper body forward, which felt anything but comfortable. And yet the excitement remained and increased even more. He asked me if it was okay with me, and I immediately said, "Yes!" And how, that was okay! I was completely in my body, feeling this mixture of excitement and security in every cell while also enjoying this feeling of helplessness, surrender, and complete trust. He knew what he was doing. He left me standing like this for a while, watching me. Then he took a vibrator out of his pocket and placed it in exactly the right place between my trouser legs. Mind you, I was still fully dressed!

It took less than thirty seconds for a huge orgasmic wave to flood my whole body. Wow! I had to laugh out loud. Mr. Magic untied me, amused, and I let myself fall into his arms, still laughing. Something like that had never happened to me before. How did it happen so quickly? He freed me from my ankle cuffs, and we went upstairs to finally drink our coffee. I had completely forgotten the time again. After the coffee, he wanted to try something else—namely, a very specific bondage variation that he once got to know in Japan. He took a long red rope out of his bag and started to wrap it artfully around my body. I crossed my arms behind my back and clasped my forearms with my hands. This was be quite comfortable, and that's a good thing because it took him almost half an hour to finish his "work of art." I couldn't move anymore, feeling like a well-tied mail package. And it arose again, that very special kind of excitement that increases with every knot. Mr. Magic asked me to lie down on the couch; it was my legs' turn. He fished a blue rope out of his pocket for this and got back to work. He obviously had a sense for the optics and explained to me later that bondage always has a beautiful appearance to it. After another quarter of an hour, he was finished and looked at his work with satisfaction. And I felt that I could hardly hold back my lust. *What is this?* I thought. *How can this be? I'm not doing anything, I'm not moving, and I'm not even being particularly stimulated.* It was just this feeling of being tied up that makes my blood boil. It's that special bodily tension I've heard about before: It didn't take long for the next orgasm to jolt through me; this time, I didn't even need a vibrator for it. I did nothing—it just came over me, even more intense than with normal sex. Madness.

As I write these lines down, I have to smile. It's 2012, the year of the six-hundred-page SM novel "Fifty Shades of Grey," which has sold millions of copies and in which the heroine experiences something similar. Someone once criticized in a review that the descriptions of her explosive climaxes were totally exaggerated. I say, No, not a bit! Whoever questions something like that has only not experienced it for themselves!

Mr. Magic was still a frequent guest with me this summer, and I enjoyed his wealth of imagination every time. I had tried many things before in the Kitty and with other men—all sorts of things, up to suspension bondage (special bondage where you float in the air). No question. But with him, it was different because it just always fit so exactly. The dream of every woman is a man who understands her without words, as if he could read thoughts. He had gained a lot of experience, obviously with many women, and he could simply feel and perceive what I liked and what I did not. I have never experienced this with another man, except maybe with Chris during the tantra massage. Mr. Magic once told me that playing the role of the dom was sometimes quite exhausting for that very reason. Because he has to concentrate so much, he says it's perfectly okay if he doesn't get to play until later, on his own. I found that really exciting. I tried out a lot of things with him that I hadn't done before in the passive role. And it was completely different again because he himself was so absorbed in his active role and that was exactly *his* thing.

When two people do together what they both love to do the most, it can only be awesome. Mr. Magic and I have been meeting and playing together regularly this summer. And I must say, most of it was much better than in my fantasy! Life Changing Sex—there it was again. Completely crazy. I was deeply frustrated by my failed relationship like I rarely have been before, and at the same time, I was experiencing the best sex of my life. Funny, isn't it?

Life, if you really get into it, is full of paradoxes. *And if everything goes your way and you feel like you can control things, that's an absolutely sure sign that you haven't gotten involved with your true life yet.*

What I also unpacked this summer, as if all that was not enough, was "Miss Susanna" as a dominatrix. That had to be. Again at a party, I met "Sub D." He was also married, a top manager in a large corporation, incredibly pleasant, educated, and simply an interesting person with whom I could talk for hours—and who dreamed of submitting to a woman. I don't think he fits the stereotype of the tough guy who gets whipped in his spare time. He was much too nice for that. He saw the whole thing more playfully and had a deep curiosity, like a little kid. An intense conversation at this party turned into a little game and, finally, the first date at my house. Now I was faced again with the question: *What do I wear? And most importantly, what do I even do with this when he comes?* But the answer came quickly. I had to smile when he stood at my door; he had come with a big box full of toys. It was amazing what he had with him! And he revealed to me that this was only one of a total of six boxes.

I could choose to my heart's content what I wanted to torture him with. Here it was again, the moment of pause. This time it was different. I hadn't experienced it like this before, the magic moment, the immersion in the here and now. Time stood still. And it was clear: I was and remained wide awake, attentive, and in service for this person. This time I would give someone else a chance to let go, to relinquish control. Because this time I set the tone.

He stood expectantly in front of me with a hungry look. First, I checked to see if he had been obedient and fulfilled my wish that he wear suspenders under his suit all day long. Yes, he was good. I ordered him to take off everything except the suspenders, and in return, I allowed him to choose one of the latex masks from the box and pull it over his face. Then I chose a pair of leather cuffs and ordered him to put them on his wrists. He thanked me, and it occurred to me that I was having a really hard time giving this man orders. I had never done this before, and the words barely found their way out of my mouth. At the same time, I was fascinated. He did everything I told him to without contradiction, and he seemed to like it. I tied him to my stair railing, got a whip out of the box, and started working his ass with it. I'm sure it was way too lax for him, but I could barely bring myself to strike harder. Being a dominatrix is really one hell of a job!

I realized at this moment what Mr. Magic meant by "You have to concentrate a lot." But Sub D was satisfied. He thanked me for every blow. I feverishly thought about what else I could do to him. I rummaged a little in his box and found a gag. I was sure he deliberately put it there, so I tried it out right away. Sub D growled contentedly, and I dared to strike harder.

Suddenly I got a very good idea: I ordered him to sit on the floor in front of me and jerk off while I watched him from above. This beat everything. It was just the right thing to do. Sub D looked at me through the eye slits of the mask, slightly horrified and totally aroused at the same time. He got going. I sensed that he was embarrassed and, at the same time, totally turned on. I threatened him with punishment if it took too long. After this command, it went fast. I watched him, fascinated. Afterward, following a refreshing shower, we went out for pizza together. We toasted with a glass of red wine, and he thanked me again for this exciting afternoon. He was happy, just beaming face. I was less excited than fascinated by the whole thing. *So that's what it's like to be a dominatrix,* I thought. What an adventure!

A dominatrix needs a lot of sensitivity and knowledge of human nature, and at the same time, strength and the courage to give very clear, concise instructions to a man and to beat him. For me, this is not easy. I don't know how other women feel. I already have a pretty tough demeanor. I decided at that time to meet Sub D more often and to practice with him. At our next appointment, he brought his second toy and clothes box.

So that summer, I had a broken heart and two affairs with married men at the same time. I didn't hold anything back, didn't hide anything anymore, and tried and lived out everything that came to my mind. At the same time, I still had a deep desire for a committed relationship and still wanted to start a family, so I met with other men on the side.

I realized that I first had to bring all my demons into the light in order to become free from what is commonly called normal. A year later, in June 2011, the time had come: I got engaged to a completely normal man, and nine months later, I was pregnant. Although it wasn't really a normal relationship. We were friends and decided quite spontaneously to get engaged and move in together. And he was also anything but normal because he had almost no experience with sex at all at that point! He had had exactly one single, short relationship before me; before that, he had been a virgin for forty years. I had tried and experienced enough and now wanted to finally really get involved with someone again and build a relationship.

We liked each other and shared many common values. He wanted children. And he wanted me. Well, and he knew what he was getting into. At least some of it.

I wrote a book about this very personal story because it was at least as crazy as the rest of my life. I was incredibly happy that I had finally found someone with whom I could share all this craziness. But it was a challenging journey, especially concerning our sex life. We started at point zero. We were not in love with each other, but we were decided for each other.

By the way, I am sure that sex in long-term relationships does not get worse but better. I was able to say that after one year, and it has been confirmed over the last few years. Long-term couples who have well-functioning and deep relationships will confirm this. You only really get to know the other person over time, you only gradually learn what he or she likes and needs, and bit by bit, you learn to give him or her that. You discover the true qualities and also the dark sides of a person—not in a few months, but gradually, over a long period of time. Everything that grows naturally takes time. Encounters like the one between Mr. Magic and I are exhilarating and they are important, but they don't build a foundation on anything. Sex in a relationship has a lot to do with trust, and that just happens to develop slowly. The prerequisite for all this is that you get involved with your partner again and again.

People lose curiosity about each other over time; that's the only reason life becomes routine. Even worse, you also lose curiosity about yourself! Boredom arises when you think you already know everything. The most brilliant thing is to discover curiosity with another person, to find out with them what makes them and *you* happy. I have found such a partner, and I am very grateful for that.

Frank and I had a very well-meaning mentor who advised us again and again for several years to give it a try together after all. At some point, the time was right, we did it quite consciously, and neither of us was in love. But we were both curious and made a decision. To find a person who gets involved in something like this is really a rarity. And how brilliant that he immediately went along with everything, accompanied me everywhere to my favorite secret places. I would *never* have expected that. Our first evening together in the swingers club, "just to look," degenerated within a short time into an orgy.

When it comes to sex, we could hardly be more different. From the outside, you could think, *Hey, that's a perfect match: someone with a lot of experience meets someone with little experience. One* can teach the other a lot, and both can learn from the other. But in fact, it wasn't that easy in bed for the two of us. Especially in this area, I didn't really want to learn anything more and I didn't want to have to teach anyone anything; I just wanted to have fun. I still needed a little patience and the willingness to do what everyone in a relationship should do: first give and then take. Frank was very eager to learn, but he still lacked the right skill. You can't learn to play the piano in a few weeks, even if you have the talent. So we practiced regularly. And I noticed something. If the feeling of being in love is missing, you can create it when you have sex regularly.

On the whole, I was relaxed and happy. I could see it as a new experience. Besides, I have found that sex is ultimately not just about having fun yourself but actually being there for your partner. I always thought it was terrible when women in relationships withheld sex from their husbands just because they didn't feel like it themselves. I had been letting off steam sexually for the past few years, experiencing everything I desperately wanted to experience. And I knew I could go get it anytime I really wanted to. So if we both needed our time to really groove on each other, that was no problem for me. I was sure it would come.

Then one Saturday afternoon at the end of October, an old acquaintance called me completely unexpectedly—let's call her Gisela. I had met her two years earlier in my favorite Munich club. She asked me if I would like to accompany her to the club that evening. The call came at just the right time. I hadn't been to the club in what felt like an eternity, and I felt that I was really missing it. Frank and I had not yet been in a club; we had so far only had sex at home. But he knew what he had gotten himself into with me. I had been wishing for an unusual experience between the two of us for a while, and it was about time. We hadn't planned anything for the evening, and I simply asked him, "How about we go to a swingers club tonight?" I thought it would be a good idea for my acquaintance to join us the first time. Then he'd have two female companions, which I was sure would be fun for him.

Frank actually said yes to the club visit pretty quickly. So we drove there, quite relaxed, with the attitude "We'll first see what we feel like doing." Since Frank had to be outfitted first, we all met at seven o'clock in the shopping center next to the club. We quickly found a casual outfit—even on that we both liked the same one. Shortly after, the three of us were standing in front of the club's door. I had a déjà vu experience: five years earlier I had stood in front of this door for the first time, incredibly excited at the time and with a man I had never seen before, a blind date in more senses than one. Mr. Darkmind. This man introduced me to the club scene back then, and with him I had one of the coolest evenings of my life. But this time I was the initiation master for Frank, who was probably as excited as I had been back then....

What I never expected in my wildest dreams resulted: We had the most fun of our lives that evening! We quickly got into conversation at the bar with a nice single man and another couple from Tyrol. Frank was totally relaxed and funny; we had a lot of fun and laughed a lot.

Between two glasses of wine, I threw the question out to the group, asking whether what I had heard the other day from a sex coach was true—namely, that men cannot kiss and women cannot blow. This started a hot discussion, and Gisela took the opportunity to test all three men on their kissing skills—and of course to prove her own mouth skills. Unfortunately, I didn't have a camera with me to capture Frank's face when Gisela pulled down the pants of the three men at the bar one after the other and briefly got down on her knees in front of them. Inconspicuously, a fourth man stood next to her. The Tyrolean and I laughed our heads off. It didn't take much longer for all seven of us to be on the second floor in one of the rooms on a mattress—a tangle of people, and in the middle a large package of body lotion. There was no sex in the strict sense, but lots of massaging hands, touching, and laughing. Some spectators came near us to watch the spectacle. I like the physical contact with several people and enjoy the action. I think people simply have to experience something like this once. Most people don't even know what they're missing otherwise! And apparently Frank liked it too—at least he didn't seem to mind. I kept glancing at him in between, and I saw that he was vigorously mixing in as if he'd never done anything else. How could I have underestimated this man so much? I would never have thought in my life that something like this was possible with him. Especially on our very first club evening together as a couple! What amazed me in particular was that he obviously had no problem at all with other men joining in. I had already been with one or the other partner or lover in such an establishment, but none of them would have accepted such a constellation. A second woman gladly, several women also, but another man? Several men? I wondered, *Is it because he does not care and is not jealous because he is not in love with me anyway? Or is it that he really likes me and just begrudges me? Or maybe it's because he doesn't even care that much about it all?* Our relationship was stable, so there was no need to worry about it. In any case, my surprise was great. Cool! Well, then life as a couple can begin!

Following is a description of the evening from Frank's point of view:

> I'm pretty excited, but I trust Susanne—she knows her stuff! I have no idea what goes on in a club like this, but I'm curious to see what happens there. I'm interested in that. Besides, I must admit I've always been curious about what it's like with several women or other couples. I've seen enough movies about that in my single days. I used to have endless fantasies in my head; I've really been alone long enough. Now I finally want to know what people do in real life, whether it's like in the movies or completely different. I just let myself go with it. There's something about the atmosphere in the club. Susanne shows me the premises, and I think to myself that nothing can happen except sex. I also briefly consider whether we should agree on any rules, how far we want to go, whether there are taboos. But the thought is quickly gone. We go to the bar and talk to a few people there. And then it gets down to business very quickly. I just let myself get carried away.
>
> I have a lot of fun. I didn't know what to expect, and I think it's cool. What I didn't expect at all and what completely surprises me is that Gisela says in her squeaky voice, "Well, I'll prove it"—and I suddenly feel her tongue in my mouth and she pulls down my boxers a few minutes later. I would not have expected that, especially because we are still standing at the bar. Wow! I have a lot of brilliant experiences that evening, and so do the others, as

far as I can tell. What I still find a bit hard to get used to are the single men who trot along behind us and want to join in. It's a good thing that I've never been alone in such a club. But Susanne has already warned me about this. My impression is that there are quite normal people here who just want to have a little fun on a Saturday night instead of watching TV. Just like us.

When we are lying on the mat with several of them, I think for a short moment whether we should have agreed on something. But stopping in the middle is stupid. This thought comes when one of the men obviously wants to have sex with Susanne. But she rejects him kindly and firmly. She only wants to have sex with her partner, that is, with me, she says to him. So that's settled, too. We don't have to agree on anything, we don't need any rules. It just fits between the two of us. Apart from that, I have no opinion about whether anything could develop between Susanne and another man. Why should it? We are both engaged and want to move in together. And Susanne likes sex. What's the problem? I think many people are stuck in the thought that they can't separate sex and love. Let's be honest: No one expects to find true love in a club. The point of sex is to try out new things and get to know other bodies. The only thing I'm really a little afraid of at the beginning is that I might fail in front of so many "witnesses." ... But that doesn't happen. So no problem.

11.11.11: My Craziest Birthday Party

In 2011, I decided to celebrate my birthday with my partner and a few friends once in a club. You have to know that I was born on November 11, and the date 11.11.11 simply invites mischief.

"Today is the craziest day of the year" was the headline of the *Bild* newspaper. True to this motto, I invited some friends to the swingers club. There were actually five curious people who wanted to share this experience with me. Two of them had never set foot in such a club before; they were a couple on the verge of separation. I advised them to try a club visit, saying maybe this adventure would bring them closer together again. And Herbert, one of my former lovers, joined in, as did Maria, who secretly supplements her household income by prostituting from time to time. And of course Gisela. That evening, we discovered the big whirlpool tub for ourselves, and I had the joy of being slicked and massaged by ten hands at the same time with a giant pack of shower gel. Is there a cooler birthday present?

We must be a little bit crazy. On the other hand, I sometimes wonder if I'm crazy or if it's the others who are, the ones who don't do stuff like we do and instead just dream about it. They spend their lives *not* doing what they really want to do and then end up feeling like they've missed the point. Well, maybe I go a bit overboard sometimes. And sometimes things don't work out the way I want them to. Then I just learn something from it. For me, these crazy actions are what make life worth living! Birthday party in a swingers club—that's something different. For my thirty-eighth birthday I got a tattoo and spent the afternoon after the procedure in an endorphin rush. That was also something. I was curious how going to the club with Frank and Herbert would be. I knew that Herbert really wanted to visit a club sometime but has never done it. And I felt like having him at my birthday party. That's why I quickly arranged for Gisela to accompany him. I didn't have to worry about Maria; she would do her thing and have fun anyway. We all met in front of the entrance, and I was pretty psyched. The evening was different from the last. I realized that I was feeling a little reserved after all. Maybe it's because I was with people I knew this time. Anonymously, it's easier for me to let loose. And I didn't know whether it would work with both Frank and Herbert. First, we all went to the bar together to drink and eat and toast my birthday. Our friends withdrew later—but others joined us. It was great fun to meet new people in this atmosphere and especially on my birthday. Every evening there is different because there are always different people, people are in different moods, and different encounters arise. With a partner it is different again. With a partner and an ex-lover, even more so! Once again I was more than amazed on this evening by how easily Frank took everything. And I felt infinitely liberated. With this man I could really do what I wanted and be who I am. He didn't slow me down or stop me, he didn't have an opinion about me, he went at the same pace as I did, and he visibly had fun doing it. I didn't have to justify myself or hold back; I could just be who I am. What a relief! I sat in beautiful black lingerie on the plush couch with a glass of white wine in front of me; next to me on one side was Frank, and on the other side was Herbert. In this moment I felt very connected to Frank, much more than I would have expected. I was happy that Herbert was also there, but I felt the connection with Frank and was really a bit in love with him that night. I don't many other men could do all this with me: birthday party at the swingers club with an ex-lover. Sitting next to Herbert, Maria started kissing him and at the same time grabbed Gisela, who was sitting on her other side, by the thigh, and the three of them sank into a wild make-out session. I watched them from the corner of my eye and was fascinated. *How easy it is here,* I thought, *in this ambience, to let go of one's inhibitions.*

After the meal and extensive toasting with prosecco, we went to the spa area and let water into the large whirlpool. I enjoyed my first water-cuddling session and intense foot massage with six other people and two bulk packs of shower gel in the club's own whirlpool. Maria explained to me that the sole of the foot has a connection to the pelvic floor, and therefore you can get an orgasm just from massaging your feet. Exciting—I did not know that yet. I stretched out both feet to her, and she skillfully pressed the right points. To the right and left of me sat my fiancé and my ex-lover, who spoiled my breasts, and I felt a few other hands on my body. I was in seventh heaven. Again, it was a real Life Changing Sex experience.

125

SubRosaDictum: A Waking Dream

Visits to fetish parties took on a new quality with my fiancé as well. There were now two of us, Frank and me. And it wasn't long before I became pregnant. The intensity and fun can always increase; there really are no limits. Although two years earlier I thought it just couldn't get any better, to this day, I'm always surprised that I enjoy it even more. As I said, it has to do with me. After my favorite club, unfortunately, closed its doors, we discovered a special event series called SubRosaDictum (www.subrosadictum.de), extraordinary fetish and BDSM parties. They always took place at changing locations, each time with a different motto. *Sub rosa dictum* means "spoken among roses." It comes from an ancient legend that says that roses were sent as an expression of secrecy in an amorous adventure. The whole thing is very discreet and very cool. The organizers wrote, "We want to create an experience that guests will remember long and with pleasure. And we want the crackle! Eroticism. Showing off. Playing, dancing, pushing boundaries." Cool! Every event was different. We entered a party location, and I felt deep peace inside me.

The bass was booming. I love it when the bass booms! I know it's not everyone's cup of tea; many even hate it, but I love it. Insider were white walls, white furniture, and a white bar, creating a spacy location with spacy music. "I like," as they like to say in the Facebook age.

We sat at the edge of the dance floor on one of those white sofas and kissed, touching each other and making out wildly like two teenagers in love who can't let go of each other. Space and time disappeared, and my brain showed a screensaver. It's actually funny that I can relax much better in the midst of so many people and with loud music than at home in my bedroom. Sometimes maybe it has to be that loud so that I can't hear my own thoughts, which otherwise run through my head all day. Just recently, at a lecture on Zen meditation, I heard that we think about forty to fifty thoughts per minute, so more than sixty thousand a day. Man, oh man, that's a lot. It's a good exercise to just let the thoughts pass by like clouds. So when I surrendered to the touches in the middle of this wacky scene all in white, between half-naked or black-gloss-clad and sweating people and with booming bass music, neither clouds nor thoughts came; my brain was switched off. I simply don't think anymore in these situations. I don't need meditation for that. It simply flows through me.

The only things that pop up in my mind's eye from time to time are memories of the last party, of other men, of other similarly bizarre situations—or perhaps of my youth, when I first sat next to the dance floor with a then-boyfriend, smooching in my favorite disco in the Sauerland. I was eighteen and had just gotten my driver's license. It was so exciting back then! The things that belong to us always come back into our lives and always feel like the first time. Meanwhile, I considered myself experienced in this scene, leaning back and relaxing. For my partner, it was rather new, but he got involved and had fun. Nothing can shock me anymore; I only get fascinated. I couldn't help grinning. I looked at the couple next to us and smiled at them. This was the first time that I did not drink alcohol at such an event. I exposed myself to this wild commotion without any mind fog. *Are people allowed to go to a fetish party while pregnant?* I wondered. *Hmm, I'll have to ask my doctor.* I sip once very lightly on the mango shooter, which is distributed to all guests, and wet my lips with it.

We went to the dance floor. I couldn't help grinning. Looking around, I saw loud people deeply immersed in the music, swaying to the twitching light rhythmically or even completely against the beat of their bodies. Right next to me was a bold-looking man with a uniform and a thick police truncheon. Next to him was an intellectual guy in a latex full-body suit with glasses and a three-day beard. At the other end of the dance floor was a two-meter Black man dressed as a drag queen with mega-high heels. What a show.

The guy with the police truncheon apologized to his neighbor because he had accidentally knocked the truncheon against his butt in a wild dance move. My grin got even wider. My newest accessory was a pair of diving goggles that quickly fogged up from the inside as I danced and sweated. I could only see everything as if through a fog, which made the whole thing even more awesome. I felt like I was in another world.

A little later, we retired to the white mattress camp and went back to our favorite activity: making out. A short time later, another couple joined us. He was in short latex shorts with a ponytail, and she was a head taller than him and had her hands tied behind her back. He had a red wand in his hand with which he sprayed sparks on her skin at irregular intervals. I had to grin again: the image of an electronic mosquito trap appeared in my mind. The wand made a similar noise. Part of me couldn't take all this seriously and kept shaking my head inwardly. The rest of me didn't care at all because it had stopped thinking. Studies have shown that women switch off large parts of their brains shortly before and during orgasm. It's been measured in magnetic resonance scanners. My orgasm lasts for a whole party, if that's what it takes. I felt only the music in my entire body, the rhythm in which we moved, and heard only now and then from the lady next door alternately lustful moans, a short *bzzzt*, and then a loud "Son of a bitch!"

After a while, we decided to interview a few people to find out what drove them to come here. First, we noticed a woman with a very special outfit of transparent plastic flowers. "This is flower wrapping foil. Made it myself; took about a week. I think of something new for every party," she said cheerfully. She had a PhD in molecular biology and revealed that she wants to win the Nobel Prize in ten years. I'd have given her right then for this her dress. She told us that she was once thrown out of an SM party because she laughed too much. I liked this woman. I would certainly get kicked out of a party for that reasons. The woman should do a cabaret. She tells me she gives lectures at university for 600 students. If only they knew what their lecturer was up to on the weekend.

Our next conversation partner was a guy in an outfit that looked as if he had come straight from a spaceship—lots of metal, silver diving goggles, thin fluorescent tubes sprouting like hair from his headgear, and green LED lights spread across his shoulders and back. He was wearing diving goggles similar to mine and said that he couldn't see much anymore and that's awesome. I could only agree with that. He came from Switzerland, and he made the outfit for himself back in Love Parade times. It was definitely a highlight at the party. I asked him whether this outfit makes him horny. He thought about it and answered that *horny* is not the right word. He felt more relaxed, explaining that he usually wore a suit and tie all day. Tall blonde women made him horny, he added.

I heard that same sentiment about relaxing from another man right after that. I asked him what he likes about these parties. Quite clearly, he said that he can relax at them. The people are all open about their bodies and their wishes and desires, and that's just a great atmosphere in which he can also let loose.

I could only agree with that! Relax, let go, and live. That's what it's all about. We didn't stay very long that evening; my circulation was not that great anymore and I felt a bit sick. I suspected that my life would change completely again in a few months.

Chapter 11

OF PRINCE CHARMING
AND FUCK BLONDES

**Men have ideas about the opposite sex that are
just as unrealistic and exaggerated as those women
have. And they have no idea what the other
actually wants. The fact that men and women
tick differently is well known, but unfortunately,
it doesn't help at all! You can't change people,
but you can teach them a lot. Because behind
all habits, we are curious and want to learn.**

The true character of a man cannot be estimated as
quickly or as easily as the size of a woman's breast.

— Sai Gaddam and Ogi Ogas

I READ A FASCINATING BOOK RECENTLY: *"A Billion Wicked Thoughts.
What the internet tells us about Sexual Relationships"* by Sai
Gaddam and Ogi Ogas. The two authors had an idea that was
as simple as it was ingenious: since it is very difficult to obtain
relevant data about people's sexuality through surveys (who tells the
truth when it comes to their own sex preferences?), the two simply

tapped into the source that is bubbling over with sex, the internet. Unobserved, men and women alike tell everything that turns them on, no matter how unusual it may be. And on the internet, there really is everything you can imagine or not imagine. The universal law of supply and demand also applies to this topic—when there is a need, suppliers will come on the scene sooner or later. In the meantime, there is almost nothing that is not available on the internet in terms of sexual material, stores, and forums—from the already mentioned wool fetishists to chastity belts (there are actually special providers for this, and the things are not even that cheap) to masturbation with barbican vacuum cleaners. And it's easy to analyze which pages are clicked on how often - even which combinations of words people enter into Google and other browsers when they're looking for something. It's even possible to find out whether a man or a woman has looked at a page by combining various software tools.

The two authors were inspired by a sociological experiment from the 1970s by psychologist Kenneth Gergen. He had five men and women, who did not know each other beforehand, enter a completely dark room one after the other and told them they could do whatever they wanted there. The room would remain dark the entire time, and at the end of the experiment, they would all never see one another again. In other words, they had 100 percent anonymity.

The participants talked to one another at first but quickly began to touch, hug, and even kiss one another. One of the men kissed all five women. Under the protection of anonymity, people quickly lose their inhibitions with others. I think a comparable phenomenon is experienced in sex clubs. It's much easier to give up inhibitions and engage in sexual encounters when you don't know the other people there and also know that you won't see them again, except perhaps in that very setting. For a long time, I have wondered why I have such a hard time convincing my many curious friends to come along just once. The reason is that they simply got to know and appreciate one another in a certain context, which usually has nothing to do with sexuality. For many, it is the horror par excellence to perhaps meet a work colleague or even the boss in such a club, so they drive long distances. Clubs near the place of residence and work are avoided for safety's sake. I was amused to meet an acquaintance from time to time. I even found it rather pleasant and humanizing, the other person being in the same situation. And quite clearly, running into each other at a fetish party means that we share a common secret that connects!

Back to the online sex report: What the two authors of this highly exciting book found out really captivated me. One important insight I gained from it is that there is one point on which men and women are amazingly similar. It is in their completely exaggerated ideas about the opposite sex.

I'm a woman, and I've always wondered why on earth men like to watch porn so much. From my point of view, most of the videos are totally exaggerated and the women are not real at all. They have pleasure at the push of a button, moan loudly just because someone rubs them, get mega orgasms in no time, love it when the men work on them with huge cocks, and behave completely unnaturally. A sex movie usually has no story and is limited to the most essential thing: close-ups. Well, men are actually more visual and look for photos and movies of naked women and sex scenes on the internet.

Speaking of dicks, by the way, they are only so clearly visible in porn because the men look at them. No joke. Women care little about looking at men's best bits. Men, on the other hand, do even if they're not gay. Men always want to know what the competition is up to.

But back to the fuck blondes. For men, this is actually something of an ideal: a woman who visibly has fun during sex, who is not afraid to flaunt her generously available feminine charms, who does not nag about anything but moans loudly with pleasure, and who simply loves everything that the man has to offer her. Especially his sperm.

Dear women, that's how men are. Every year they
click over 100 million times on porn sites.

Men want pictures. That's why *Playboy* has existed since 1953. *Playgirl* is read primarily by gay men. As a rule, women can do little with pictures alone. They tick differently, think differently, and react to different stimuli. But what is it that really turns women on? What women are looking for on the internet is prince charming on a white horse. (Now, probably all men who read this book will develop flight instincts.) Most clicks from women land on romance novels! It's hard to believe, but every year, almost as many websites with romance novels are visited as porn sites. The days of *Julia* and *Baccara* magazines at the grocery store next door are over. Today, women can read them online or on their e-readers in the morning on the subway. That's much better because no one sees them there. And the ladies pay a lot for them. Men are known to be willing to pay for sex. It's always been that way and probably always will be. Women pay for romance novels. At the top of the list is so-called fan fiction. Female authors are writing erotic stories about pirates, robbers, criminals, and well-known heroes like Harry Potter, Adrian Monk, and Captain Kirk in droves.

What fascinates me, particularly, is that so-called slash literature is extremely popular in this genre. Here, romantic and sexual encounters develop between two male heroes, such as Captain Kirk and Mr. Spock or Harry Potter and Draco Malfoy. It's hard to believe that such stories are both written and read by women! Obviously, women like stories about homosexual sex between men with one caveat—only if the two are actually soulmates.

I recently read *Fifty Shades of Grey*. I had to. Even though I don't usually read romance novels, this work made me curious. And indeed, I could hardly stop reading, not necessarily because of the sex scenes, something I had already experienced live. What fascinated me was the dream image of all women about men that is rarely brought *so* well to the point. No wonder the thing sells millions of copies!

The hero is a young billionaire, a top alpha male who is tough, clever, outrageously good-looking, always sexily dressed, eloquent, opaque, and superior and who knows exactly what he wants—until the moment he meets the heroine. Then he suddenly becomes insecure, soft, and affectionate. Of course, he always lets her feel his strong hand and dominant leadership, but he opens up bit by bit and gradually shows her his soft core. This is only for her, of course, because she is very special. He desires her, the inconspicuous, shy and, inexperienced student who constantly bites her lip uncertainly. No other woman interests him more, not even her attractive best friend.

I bet that every man who reads something like this will wonder if women are into guys with personality disorders. And he will say that this behavior is completely exaggerated and unrealistic and no man can ever live up to it.

> *Dear men, that's how women are. Every year, they read an estimated 84 million romance novels on the internet. And* Fifty Shades of Grey *had already sold more than 100 million copies worldwide as of 2014.*

When it comes to love and sex, women ultimately have ideas about men that are just as unrealistic as those men have about women. And if you take a deep and honest look inside yourself, you will confirm that this is indeed the case. While reading *Fifty Shades of Grey*, I kept thinking, *Yes, that's it. He's a dream guy. I want a man like that. Oh, if only my husband were like him.* We can't prevent ourselves from thinking such things. It is deeply anchored in our genes. Women want men who can provide for them and protect them, who are not mama's boys, and who provide the best possible genes for their offspring. It sounds like a cliché, and it is. And it is the truth.

What's hard for women to believe is that men compare much less than women. Men love all breasts and all pussies. A man usually doesn't think, *Oh, if only my wife was like the woman in the porn!* They just watch the movies to relax and because it's fun, to inspire themselves. Or because their wives won't let them at home. By the way, most women don't just hate it when their husbands watch porn; they also think it's a bad idea. They consider it a real disaster.

If *she* catches *him* looking at porn, there's a huge drama: "Why do you need these fuck blondes? Am I not enough for you?" I don't think a man would ever ask his wife if he's still enough for her when she's reading a novel. Men can't understand our excitement at all because, conversely, they would be totally turned on by their wives watching porn. The online sex report also found this out. Most men would love to watch porn with their partners to get each other hot. For many gay men, catching the other guy watching porn is the hottest turn-on. And as I said, men love pictures. This reminds me of a lover a few years ago who once asked me to take pictures of my pussy with my cell phone and send them to him via text message. This request was met with quite a bit of incomprehension from me at the time, just like his offer to text me photos of his best piece in return. Why would I have wanted something like that? We just tick differently. I think we women should stop judging men for loving fuck blondes and porn. We shouldn't resent them for liking to look at other women's bouncing breasts, just like they shouldn't resent us for reading tearjerker novels. In a way, they're both really the same thing: It just feels good and helps us relax. To dream and indulge in your desires once in a while is wonderful. And accepting that real life is the way it is makes it easy. Sex makes you healthy also in this way. And the bottom line is that, from relaxation, it's much easier to make your partner curious and win him over to fulfilling your desires.

Here's what we can actually do: *Women can make their men heroes.* Dear women, give your men more recognition. Stop nagging at them! Rather, tell them what you want and teach them bit by bit. Men grow beyond themselves when they can make women happy. We just don't let them most of the time. *And men can spoil their women* so that they get pleasure from sex. Women so often don't enjoy sex because men just don't make an effort and the sex is boring. Dear men, try harder. Women love to surrender and be pampered. And they love men who take the initiative.

Chapter 12

SEX IS WOMEN'S BUSINESS—
MEN HAVE NO IDEA ABOUT IT!

**Even if good sex has a lot to do with the right
technique, women have the greater talent
for it. How women teach men good sex.**

A woman's most precious possession
is a man's imagination.

— Beate Uhse

"YOU DON'T TALK ABOUT MONEY; you have it." This sentence is
more likely to be said by a man. "You don't talk about sex;
you have it" is certainly more likely to come from the mouth of a
woman. The fact that men make so many jokes about sex may be
because they don't actually know anything about it. The good news
is that women can teach them.

The best lovers who ever made me happy were those who had
many other women before me and who, during our first encounters,
concentrated exclusively on me and my reactions and didn't want
to get any action themselves. In sexual relationships with all other
men, I very often asked myself, *Why can't he just do it the way I
like it?* In the beginning, I admit, maybe I didn't say what I liked at

136

all. I actually had the idea for quite a long time that the man would have to come up with it himself by simply observing my reactions. I have—from my perspective—shown clearly enough what I like and what I don't like. Has it brought anything? Not a bit of it!

Men can't read minds. Not everyone observes. And empathy is not the main talent with which men are born. For example, when one man started rubbing again, I said loudly and clearly, "Ow, not so hard!" I always thought that should be enough. If I say "not so hard," then he should know to do it more gently. Is that not so? But the next time, it was the same problem.

Later, I wondered, *Maybe it's unusual that I like it slow and gentle during sex? Maybe I'm a special case. In porn, intercourse is always a pretty fast-paced thing. And if women really like that kind of thing, I must be an exception.* Years later, I read something about "boy sex" and "girl sex" that reassured me I wasn't alone in that after all. At some point, I started to tell my men what I like: "*Slooow* movements."

Saying that was a real overcoming for me at first. Women generally don't talk about sex, especially not with their partners. I think that's hard for many women. He's got to hear about it, darn it! The easiest way is certainly with humor. I once read something funny in a sex guidebook: Many women don't like it when a man moves his fingers or tongue like a woodpecker—pointed, fast, in, out. I told my partner that, and he understood immediately. Later, however, I had to realize that it was not enough to say something like that only once because boys often forget it in the heat of the moment. But it doesn't matter; today I only have to say, "The woodpecker is back!" and we both laugh. It's also not enough to just tell a man what we women *don't* want. We have to explain and show him exactly what we *do* want. When we first learn to knit, we can't do it well the first time, either! Some places offer knitting courses and instructions, and you have to go there several times before you can make a great sweater. Practice makes perfect. Sex is actually a handcraft, in the truest sense of the word.

Dear women, have you ever told your husband how you like sex best? Very specifically? Where and how exactly should he touch you? How gentle or firm do you like it best? What makes you horny?

Men know what they like themselves: mostly simple, fast, and uncomplicated. And they naturally assume that we are just like them. They have far fewer demands than women. Maybe that's because they touch their most important sexual organs daily on the toilet and are much more familiar with their little friends than women are with their little girlfriends. Women often don't even know what they look like "down there." Men have a simple on switch for sex, and they respond to even a single stimulus with a physical and mental erection. Tits, butt, pussy, a pretty face with bright red lips, long hair, or whatever turns a man on—one signal is enough. That's it. The rest doesn't matter. Sai Gaddam and Ogo Ogas call this "the Power of Or" in their online sex report: tits *or* ass *or* pussy. By the way, it is quite natural that men like to stare after women on the street. This has now even been measured with brain scans: Positive feelings arise in the control center of men when they look at pretty women.

With women, it's all much more complicated. It starts with the fact that they have an on and an off switch. And with them, a simple stimulus is not enough to get sexually aroused. The law of *and* applies to them: they need several stimuli at once, for example, a good-looking man *and* a pleasant smell *and* subdued light *and* touches in the right place *and* maybe some nice music. In this context, it is also interesting that women with a strong sex drive are attracted to men *and* women *and* different types of play. Men with a strong sex drive are more interested in what corresponds to their sexual orientation, that is, straight *or* gay *or* fetish.

Women are much more complex, diverse, and demanding during sex than men. If something doesn't fit, the excitement is quickly gone. As I said, we also have an off switch. Woe to the man who accidentally presses it! What makes the whole thing more difficult is that women often don't even realize that they are aroused. There was an experiment in which Canadian scientists showed men and women various short film scenes and simultaneously measured their arousal on their genitals. The test subjects were each shown a sports scene with men or women, a sex scene with a straight couple, one with a gay couple, one with two women, and one with two monkeys. The results showed that the men were only aroused during the sex scene that corresponded to their own sexual preference. And they were aroused both psychologically and physically. Straight men were aroused by the straight couple and the two women. In contrast, the film clips with the gays and the monkeys and the sports sequences did not turn the test subjects on at all. Gay men were turned on by the gay scene.

A completely different result came to light for the women. The measurement indicated physical arousal in all (!) scenes, but the women claimed that none (!) of the scenes had turned them on. Apparently, there is a big gap between women's actual arousal and their feeling of being aroused. This may explain why women often don't feel like having sex at first but do enjoy it once they get going. As the saying goes, appetite comes with eating. This seems to apply to women in particular. What's more, women's appetites are changing.

What was good yesterday does not necessarily work today. If a man does not get on with his "program," then he is quickly at a loss unless he has developed imagination and sensitivity and learned to be attentive and a good lover. Or the woman simply decides to have fun and get involved, even if she doesn't feel like it just yet. Girls, relax—it will come!

Sex is a woman's thing! *Because women are the bottleneck, if the woman doesn't have fun, the man doesn't either. Then there are bitching, nagging, and bad moods .*

Sex is women's business because women are naturally more empathetic and flexible, more likely to give in, and more connected to their bodies. Women are actually naturals when it comes to sex. It's just that, in our sex-hostile culture, religion, and upbringing, as well as centuries of oppression of women, this talent has not been allowed to develop. And that sits deep. Women are actually, by their nature, pure sensuality. Their sexual drive may not be as strong, but when it comes down to it, women are the ones who provide quality. If it's not like that with you, you see where the patriarchy has brought us.

The fact is that women pretty quickly figure out what pleases the men in their lives simply because they are more sensitive and recognize men's signals faster. What they do then is another question. For men, on the other hand, how to satisfy women is a great mystery and perhaps one of the most important questions of their lives. It's a challenge they want to solve but often can't because we women don't tell them clearly what we enjoy and they don't know how else to find out. How is a man supposed to know what a woman likes? That women are different and that each wants something different, they have already noticed. Men want clear messages from us. What they do not know is that most women are incredibly embarrassed to talk openly about sexual fantasies and desires.

What woman would readily admit that she would like to be taken or called a slut just once? Women do not, or rarely, say such things, especially not to their beloved partners who have just put the children to bed. Nevertheless, we women have to give men instructions on how to use their skills, especially if they don't have much experience yet. And we have to be patient with them. You don't become a piano virtuoso in a week; it takes years. The good news is that we can be sure that once a man has found a good way to satisfy us, he will do it again and again. The most important thing women should do if they want to teach their man something is to give him credit and praise him for his progress. Men need *much* more recognition than women do. If a woman feels she is overdoing it with compliments, that's when it gets interesting for the man. Just try it out, even if it is difficult for you at first. You will see; your man will lay the world at your feet. (A great book recommendation for this is *Hello Tarzan,* really the best and most honest book I have ever read on the subject of relationships!)

The Real Differences Between Men and Women—
From the Perspective of Transsexuals

I was fascinated one day by a conversation with an acquaintance who talked about her relationship with a trans man. A trans man is a woman who lives as a man, a transsexual. Such a relationship must be very exciting, and I found this conversation extremely exciting. After all, where else would I get to see firsthand how different men and women really are? This trans man of my acquaintance decided against hormone therapy and gender reassignment but otherwise lived as much as possible as a man. Hormone therapy is quite intense, I learned that evening, and that's why many transsexuals discontinue it. What happens when a woman takes the male hormone testosterone for a long time? It must be similar to a boy whose body is flooded with hormones at the onset of puberty and who no longer knows what is happening to him. And he already had testosterone in his blood before. This hormone causes the body to become more masculine and the voice deeper, fat shifts from the hips to the belly, and muscles and body hair increase, as do physical performance and the desire for sex. What happens psychologically? Testosterone makes people aggressive. The trans man suddenly feels aggression that he has never experienced before as a woman. Men—even the most harmless ones—have a literal killer instinct. Many women don't know that. The hormone not only makes people more aggressive, it also increases their sex drive. They suddenly have a constant desire. I read somewhere that men feel horniness about seven times more than women. What also happens through testosterone therapy is that the person becomes more self-centered and selfish. And, the worst for many women in transition to men, they lose their intuition and empathy and look as if through a tunnel.

Aggressive, horny, self-centered, dull—are men really like that compared to women? Of course, this varies from person to person, but it cannot be completely dismissed. Conversely, what happens to men who want to become women and take estrogen, the female hormone? Physically, their skin becomes softer, fat shifts to the hips and buttocks, the musculature recedes, and physical performance decreases. At the same time, the sex drive is dampened, and the trans woman has much less desire than before. Many trans women also drop out of therapy because they can't stand the fact that they become so emotional, suffer from mood swings, and often have to cry.

Emotional and moody—are women really like that compared to men? There is certainly something to this as well. Women with an unfulfilled desire to have children who are undergoing hormone therapy can also confirm this. As a friend of mine described it once, "I used to cry when I couldn't find a parking space!" And, yes, it is indeed due to the hormones. My friend stopped the therapy and then got pregnant naturally.

Chapter 13

SEX RELAXES ANNOYED WOMEN

Every man knows the saying, "The bitch has to be fucked properly." Doctors knew more than a hundred years ago that there is a lot of truth in that.

The meaning of life is to somehow bridge
the time between two orgasms.

— Katie Price

A GOOD VIBRATOR SHOULD BE PART of every woman's standard nightstand drawer contents, whether she's in a relationship or not. Allegedly, every third woman in Austria owns a vibrator; in Germany, every fifth; and in the United States, almost half of the women. But despite enlightened times, there are certainly still far too few. I can't help but think of a participant in one highly interesting dildo-Tupper evening who snidely said she didn't need such a thing; after all, she had a healthy hand. "Sure, no problem," said the dildo saleswoman. "With a carriage, you get along quite well. But with a race car, it makes it much more fun and goes faster." She was right.

There are many types of orgasms in women. The one triggered

by vibration is quite ingenious and actually happens in no time—one to a few minutes, and voilà! Perfect, if a woman wants it to go quickly.

What is quite forgotten is that the vibrator was originally invented by a doctor who treated hysterical women with it. No joke. Until the beginning of the nineteenth century, hysteria was still officially considered a woman's disease, the symptoms of which could be temporarily relieved by producing a "hysterical paroxysm," or spasm (i.e., an orgasm, but they didn't call it that back then). Hysteria was widespread. Symptoms such as insomnia, depression, overexcitability, sexual fantasies, crying fits, and many others were attributed to hysteria. Some doctors even claimed hysteria was as widespread as the common cold. It was clear that this was a purely female disease, and it was thought to be somehow caused by the uterus. Since, at that time, people had no idea about hormones and no one officially had the idea that a woman could, after all, help herself, the most important advice to hysterical women was to get married and have many children as soon as possible.

The midwives and doctors treated hysteria by special water jet therapy or by manual massages of the female genitals. The latter was quite strenuous and not so easy to learn. In the 1880s, London doctor Mortimer Granville developed the first electric vibrator, which made it possible to solve this problem much faster. His story is greatly depicted in the movie *Hysteria*. Granville developed tennis elbow pretty quickly in the movie version from the job. In fact, he mastered it quite well, and the women were soon lining up in front of his practice. There had already been mechanical approaches from the United States for machines that could trigger the hysterical paroxysm—for example, a so-called manipulator that was operated with steam and ultimately did not catch on because it was simply too big and noisy and someone always had to push coals after it.

In any case, doctors and patients breathed a sigh of relief when this new and uncomplicated fast "healing method" powered by electric current and later by batteries came into use. In the 1920s, vibrators appeared more and more frequently in pornographic contexts and were then taboo in medicine. Hysteria was also no longer considered a disease requiring treatment. Today it is no longer socially acceptable to speak of "hysterical women," yet it is immediately clear to everyone what it means. And I think it is also understandable to everyone that sex is a good antidote.

There is no denying that women relax through sex. There is nothing like a good orgasm! Ultimately, everyone relaxes through sex. Men know this and simply lay hands on themselves more often. There's nothing wrong with it for them; they touch their best pieces themselves several times a day anyway, and they know that this is a way to get rid of pressure. But unfortunately, it's often different for women. They have much less relation to their pleasure center down there, and depending on how they were brought up, this relation is neutral or downright negative. Get rid of the pressure in this way? How is that supposed to work?

Sex Is a Matter of the Body

Just as we give our bodies nourishment, exercise, and care, we should also give them pleasure, no matter whether we have partners or not.

It's simple: express your aggression once through the channel "sex," physically and verbally. For example, go a little harder at your partner, move more, moan loudly, or even scream. You should come in any case to the "relaxation spasm," even if you worry about it yourself. *He* likes to watch. All this pleases your partner a thousand times better than if you nag him while in a bad mood!

Let's get back to the topic of the vibrator. Vibrations promote blood circulation and are excellent for sexual stimulation. Vibrators come in a wide variety—big, small, fast, slow, and infinitely adjustable—and you can stimulate all kinds of body parts with them. I find the Tantra Beam particularly exciting; my fiancé and I bought it at an erotic fair. It's a vibration transmitter, a small device that you strap around your finger and that makes your whole hand vibrate slightly. Being stroked with it is awesome! Definitely worth trying it out once.

The "nation's love servant," Beate Uhse, was a pioneer in

sexual freedom, education, and sex toys. With her company, she revolutionized the entire subject of sexuality. What particularly fascinated me is that, in the beginning, Uhse really wanted to educate only women who simply had no idea at all about sexuality in the 1950s. In the uncertain and poor economic times after the war, many did not want to have children under any circumstances but did not know how to prevent it. They didn't even know for sure how children were made in the first place; many thought it would happen when they kissed. Uhse's first "product" was Script X, a couple of notes explaining natural contraception. A little later, she added condoms to her assortment, and over time, more and more "articles for marital hygiene" expanded her range. As gratefully as many women accepted her information and products, envious people, philistines, and enemies quickly appeared on the scene. In the course of her life, Uhse had to conduct close to two thousand court cases, of which she lost only one. Legendary is a trial from 1969, in which not only Beate Uhse with her company but the orgasm itself was on trial.

The word *orgasm* comes from Greek and means "abounding fullness." According to Section 184 of the german criminal code, at the time, sex-related products and aids to artificially enhance the orgasm were not permitted, because it was lewd: this was understood to mean anything that served to "unnaturally increase sexual stimuli." Beate Uhse's nubbed, grooved, and pronged condoms; blood circulation-enhancing creams; and several other articles fell under this reproach. It was said that these things would cause a particularly strong orgasm, and this was considered fornication according to some ancient law from the empire. In total, this trial lasted three years and was finally decided in the federal court: Orgasm was acquitted with the reasoning that there can be, medically, no unnatural increase of the orgasm in itself. Climax is climax. Everything that would help to reach it was good. After all, it was already undisputed at that time that an orgasm promotes health. Furthermore, a forensic doctor noted that partnerships would probably not suffer from too much but rather from too little sexuality. Awesome! All this was not so long ago—1969. It's almost impossible to imagine today. That was the time when our parents were young. The name Beate Uhse is now known to almost everyone. For most people, it refers to sex stores. For me, it also refers to a courageous woman who had a vision and fought for it.

Where do we really stand on the subject of sex today? Where do you stand? How free are you?

Which Dildo Suits Me?

Interview with Aksana Rasch, intimacy coach and former toy consultant (https://aksana-rasch.de)

Aksana, you organized many evenings for women on the topics of sexuality, femininity, lust, and love, and you also presented sex toys. What exotic or fancy toys do you know?

There is really everything nowadays; you can let your imagination run wild. From nub dildos to stimulation current, you can get everything in all variations. For example, dildos: There are some that are particularly large, hard, soft, thick, simple or artfully designed, long or mini dildos in a lipstick format. I find vegetable dildos funny. What would you try once? Corn, eggplant, or rather a gherkin? What fascinates me in particular: Some are so big that I really think, *What, that's supposed to fit in your butt?* For example, there's the Eleven, a stainless steel dildo that weighs 1.2 kilograms. Not for beginners and the untrained.

Are there also toys that can be used together with your partner?

Yes, of course, many women asked me about it. Actually, the partner can be integrated with all toys, because which man would say no when he can watch his partner bring herself lustfully by hand or with a vibrator in ecstasy? There are no limits to the imagination. What I find ingenious for both at the same time: the "We-Vibe vibrator." The woman inserts it and it stimulates both vaginally and clitorally, and at the same time, the partner can still penetrate with it. I must say that is just awesome; I use it often myself!

What do you recommend for beginners? What is the best thing to buy first?

The VAKS rule applies: Vibrator, Angenehm, Klein, Silikon (vibrator, pleasant, small, and made of silicone.) For many women, the topic of orgasm is still a big question mark. It is widely discussed in the media and there are thousands of descriptions, but the fact is that many women do not know when they have an orgasm and how it feels. With a vibrator, it's usually very easy.

Many women do not know when they have an orgasm?

There are evenings when women say directly, "I have never had an orgasm." If that happens right at the beginning, then the ice is broken and the other women realize that there is no danger of losing face. They can let loose and talk it out with the others. What does an orgasm feel like? We all look different, by the way, including our private parts, so why should orgasm feel the same for everyone? There are orgasms at different levels and with different intensities. Clitoral, vaginal, anal, G-spot, maybe even just touching the skin in certain places is enough to feel a tingling, throbbing, explosion, or whatever. This is a taboo subject that women don't usually talk about. I often experience this in my evenings when women come out and dare to talk openly. Especially when I'm in the villages, those who come want to talk honestly. Once I was in a place that my navigation system couldn't even find, it was so small. The hostess had invited fifteen friends; they were all thrilled and we laughed in tears.

Do women really talk openly with each other about sex? Between girlfriends?

If one of them starts it, the others join in 90 percent of the time. Example: One of the women says, "I like doing anal." Then the reactions are initially fierce: "What, you like that? How crazy is that?" But the topic is out, and everyone discusses it. The conversations then run all by themselves, and I actually just moderate.

I'm sure there are many who are afraid to say anything in the group.

Of course. They tend to listen, and that's okay. Sometimes I have evenings where very little is said, there's a rather restrained atmosphere, and hardly anyone asks questions. Interestingly, a lot is ordered anyway. I offer everyone the opportunity to talk to me again on their own after the event. In these conversations, I have received the best feedback and a great deal of gratitude for what they have learned. In my evenings I always wanted to awaken the desire and curiosity to play. What's always a lot of fun for everyone: practicing how to touch a cock and pussy, very practically, on silicone models. Most women have little to no connection to their vaginas. We don't learn that anywhere. On the other hand, we live in an ingenious time in which we finally come to terms with our bodies, especially our private parts.

What kind of topics women like to talk about?

Sexuality in old age, dildo slip, is it fun? Or multiple orgasms. The latter, by the way, is a very frequent topic, along with oral sex. Other examples are falling in partnership or self-love and acceptance of my own body. Sometimes there are also questions like, "Oversized labia, am I normal?" There are many question marks on the subject of lube: pleasure-enhancing lubes, washing silicone lube out of the wash, lube without stains, or anal cramping gel.

Does it actually work to use an anal decongestant gel?

This numbs the sphincter muscle. But the real letting go and unclenching begins in the head. Try to let go inwardly and open up. The willingness comes from within; it is an inner letting go. Communication between the two partners plays a very important role. Rules that are set beforehand must be followed; otherwise the fun will be gone before it has even started. If you don't relax in your head, you can rub yourself with all sorts of things, but it won't do any good. For me, it's different every time. It depends a lot on how well I can let go at that moment. It also doesn't help if I know that I've already done that many times.

What are the differences in lubricants?

There are silicone-based, oil-based, and water-based lubricants. Silicone-based lubricants should not be used with silicone and also not with condoms because silicone "rubs" on silicone and the material becomes porous. Always use water-based gels with a toy. This is the rule of thumb so that the pleasure of the toy can work for a long time.

What do you use silicone gel for then?

This is brilliant for "slip parties" or massages because it does not absorb into the skin as quickly as water or oil. There are also special sheets for the bed. You can simply slide around with your whole body.

What is actually the difference between a dildo and a vibrator?

There is a striking difference—a vibrator has an engine and vibrates, and a dildo does not vibrate. A vibrator is perfect for stimulating the female pleasure point, the clitoris, so quickly and effectively that woman can explode within seconds. Meanwhile, the motors are so powerful that women go off like a rocket. It's a great way to experiment. Do I want a curvature to reach the G-spot, or do I like grooves, nubs, or rather smooth? What do I like? You have to work with a dildo yourself. I would say dildos are for advanced users. And, of course, also for the anal area. The advantage is that you can take it with you into the bathtub! Most vibrators, on the other hand, are not waterproof. And you can take the dildo anywhere else and use it everywhere because it makes no noise at all.

I heard there are also dildos made of wood.

The main material for vibrators and dildos is medical silicone, but there are also glass, stainless steel, sandstone, and even wood. Wood is a very natural material. It doesn't give way, it's hard, but it's very pleasant and warm when you touch it. It also has a unique smell. The surface is either natural, in which case it feels velvety, or it is highly polished and sealed with piano lacquer, as in instrument making. This creates a mirror-smooth surface. A person who is very close to nature may be attracted to wood. This is where the research journey begins as to which material appeals to one personally.

You recommend picking the perfect vibrator with the "nose test."

Exactly, you hold the vibrator to your nose, so you have an idea of how it feels when you stimulate the clitoris in the genital area. You can also try it on the palm of your hand, in the crook of your elbow, or on the back of your knee. From this, you will get a feeling for the strength of the vibration.

What are your personal insider tips?

My secret tip is to really *play* with things. Who says that adults only have to work, solve problems, and fulfill their duty? For a long time I had no idea about a fulfilling sex life. What is an orgasm? Why do people even think of putting things in their butts? Why get tied up and hung upside down? And what on earth is it about sex toys? In February 2009, I hosted a sex toy party myself for the first time, and that was a lot of fun for me. A little later, I had my first vibrators, several of them. I read the first books on the subject of masturbation, which was also not in vogue with me before. My favorite is still Betty Dodson's *Sex for One*, a must for every woman who wants to have fun with herself. I got an idea of what an orgasm felt like for the first time in my life. And just a short time later, I became a sex toy consultant myself.

What turns you on the most?

I like to involve my whole body and touch and feel myself during the act. Hearing the breath slowly turn into gasps and moans and feeling the air in the room start to crackle. Allowing the feeling of, "I'm hot and I want sex. Now!" What I also like to do is imagine what would turn me on, what places I'd like to have sex, so taking on the role of director and turning on my head cinema first. And then experience things for real. Example: the quickie in the locker room. At first, I imagined it in all colors, and then at some point, it happened. My partner brought me the lace thongs in the lingerie store in Munich, and then there was no stopping me. The dressing room was really nice and big and had a thick curtain. Of course, we then also bought something. Speaking of the film, I can highly recommend women the porn of Petra Joy. She has set the female head cinema really ingeniously in the scene, away from the mainstream porn films. Great pornographic films that give inspiration and courage to set your own head cinema in motion.

There are women who ask their husbands if they can buy a sex toy.

When I ask the women after my evenings who would like to order, quite often, the answer comes, "I have to ask my husband first" or "I don't know if my husband likes it." Then I say, "Girls, you don't ask your husband if you should go to the hairdresser either, do you? You just do it!" This is about women and what they want and how they can feel pleasure. This has nothing to do with the man at first. The women become more relaxed, calmer. The man is happy about that; you don't have to discuss it with him beforehand.

What is your most important message to women?

Try things out in the area of sexuality! Dare! Stand by what you want to experiment with! Treat yourself! We go to the cinema and spend money, we visit the hairdresser, get our nails done, buy clothes, everywhere we invest money. Invest in your sexuality and yourself, and buy a good sex toy. Personally, I once bought a really expensive toy made of stainless steel, and with it, I had my first G-spot orgasm. My partner guided the part, and I could completely let myself go. That was awesome! And a good friend of mine has now copied me—after five years! She has bought an anal chain and a very noble and expensive vibrator. She used to laugh at the subject, and now she has finally dared to do it. And she did it without asking her husband.

I say thank you for this inspiring interview

Chapter 14

SEX KILLS WRINKLES

Sex is one of the best anti-aging remedies and has no side effects. Dark circles, fat rolls, and wrinkles can simply be "fucked away" and with great fun. Sex makes you happy and healthy—and sometimes dumb. Interesting facts from research and science.

Anything that's fun keeps you young.

— Curd Jürgens

THE FIVE L'S—LIVING, LIKING, LAUGHING, learning, and loving— are generally considered the most natural and best antiaging measures. Then you don't need expensive wrinkle creams and certainly no more cosmetic surgery. Most people still run and enjoy themselves from time to time, but not everyone is there anymore when it comes to learning. We adults laugh only a few times a day, if at all. And love? Many scientists have already discovered that sex is purely antiaging. A neuropsychologist from the Royal Edinburgh Hospital recently came to this conclusion in a study: People who have sex an average of three times a week look up to ten years younger!

During sex, a lot of happiness hormones are released, which have a positive effect on the organism. At the same time, stress hormones are released more quickly and the cells' ability to absorb important vital substances is improved. Even good old Martin Luther is said to have called for regular sex: "Twice in a week, makes in the year a hundred and four, harms neither you nor her!"

We Germans aren't doing too badly there. According to the Sex Report 2008, the largest sex survey in Germany with almost 56,000 respondents, Germans have sex an average of 2.6 times a week. Allegedly, 50 percent of women and a good 60 percent of men would like more frequent sexual intercourse. And just under 40 percent of both sexes have been unfaithful at some point.

By the way, what I also find very interesting in this context is an American study that deals with the question "Why do people have sex at all?" The scientists came up with 237 reasons, including the following, during their research:

- I wanted to show my love. (women)
- I was hot. (men)
- I wanted a promotion. (women)
- I wanted to end my partnership. (men)
- I wanted to feel closer to God. (women)
- I found out that I am in love. (men)

By far, the most frequently cited reason for sex for both men and women is, "I felt attracted to the other person." Relatively high on the list for both sexes is also, "It happened in the heat of the moment." Curiously, rather low on the list was, "It was a rite of passage for a club or organization." What kind of club might that be where people have to have sex? Another interesting result of this study is that quite a few women have sex to get rid of their headaches. Well, dear women, this excuse will no longer count in the future. There is actually a study that clearly shows that sex helps against migraines.

What I can now confirm from my own experience is that everything that has to do with sexuality and pregnancy makes you young! Being pregnant is a true fountain of youth for a woman since, during this time and in the subsequent breastfeeding period, hormones are released in heaps that not only increase feelings of happiness but also regenerate brain and organ cells. That's actually true. Lately, people have been asking me when I took the photos on my website because I look a lot younger now. The many laugh lines that were around my eyes are as good as gone. Back to sex, the orgasm is a firework of hormones! Prolactin is a hormone that is normally released in a woman's body when breastfeeding. Interestingly, men produce more of it during orgasm. It is responsible for the fact that the guys are so relaxed and sleepy *after* sex and just feel good. Oxytocin is the main bonding hormone. It causes us to become emotionally attached to the person we have sex with or to form an emotional bond after sex. Incidentally, oxytocin is released in its highest concentration when a child is born.

Could oxytocin be the scientific explanation that some women say that the birth of a child is actually a huge orgasm? Incidentally, oxytocin has a stronger overall effect on women than on men. Men have fewer binding sites for this hormone, and in addition, its effect is weakened by the male sex hormone testosterone. In fact, men find it easier to have sex simply for the sake of having sex, without a relationship. Oxytocin, by the way, is considered a "softener" for men because it also strengthens their ability to bond. Unfortunately, few practical ways have yet been found for women to administer it to their husbands. The researchers have it easy; they simply take a special nasal spray. However, some studies also say that oxytocin makes men stupid and they have a demonstrably poorer memory after orgasm, which is also not to be dismissed out of hand.

Other researchers claim to have found out that hormones are released during a man's orgasm that form new brain cells. And, of course, a whole army of scientists is researching means to increase pleasure. Interestingly, so far, there is no real working pleasure-increasing drug for the female sex. Viagra for women was a failure because, for them, just improving blood flow to the genitals is not enough. They have to be aroused first, and as we have already seen in previous chapters, this is not so simple. So far, the only thing that has shown an effect in women is a substance that directly targets the pleasure centers in the brain. It was originally designed as an active ingredient for self-tanners, and so far, it has not been released on the market. What is, in any case, pleasing is that hardly any other activity consumes as many calories as intensive lovemaking. So sex is always good for losing weight as long as you get plenty of exercise. Speaking of losing weight, a study conducted during the 2012 Olympics investigated whether sex before their competitions is good for competitive athletes or not. The results were clear: For athletes competing in sports where concentration is required, *yes*. Shooters benefit from hanky-panky the night before. Power athletes and sprinters, on the other hand, are better off practicing abstinence because their aggression and strength potential is higher without having sex.

Chapter 15

NO MORE BURNOUT— BRING ON SEX

Why isn't sex available on prescription for burnout, depression, and other issues? Problems that arise in the head are better solved through the body. But sex often doesn't work, either. Why both burnout and sexual disorders are more common in sex-hostile societies.

It's nonsense that men always think about sex.
Only when they think do they think about sex.

— Geri Halliwell

B URNOUT IS ON EVERYONE'S LIPS—THE fashionable new disease of the twenty-first century. Being overtaxed by one's job and by one's life—incidentally, often a well-disguised underchallenge called bore-out—is spreading and captivating more and more people. According to *Handelsblatt* and *Manager Magazin*, large companies report almost 9 percent of employees are suffering from burnout. The consequences for those affected are often depression and a deep dislike of life. While it was still "in" in the nineties to work especially hard, today, people are trying again to find a balance in life between job, family, and their own vitality. Easier said than done. Where do you start? Most people try to organize their many tasks and activities better, engage in elaborate time and life management, write appointments with the family in their overflowing calendars, keep to a diet, participate in sports, regularly go to relaxation classes and maybe even to a psychiatrist, and ultimately cause themselves even more stress with everything. When I go for a walk along the Isar on the weekend and the rushed managers race past me on their mountain bikes at breakneck speed, I sometimes ask myself whether this promotes balance. But even the calmer types of exercise are apparently not suitable for everyone. Studies of heart rate variability—a very good indicator of stress and vitality—have shown that yoga actually brought about relaxation in only about 50 percent of the test subjects. The others tended to become even more aggressive as a result. So how do you achieve balance and peace? You can do that only by strengthening your own resources.

Performance Ultimately Comes Only from Passion

And you can feel it in your body. People who feel pleasure, joy, and passion in their activities don't have to work so hard. If you do things you want to do as often as possible, you automatically tap into your resources repeatedly and your power doesn't run out. From my point of view, there are two ways to strengthen your resources. One is to find out what really relaxes you and gives you energy, and that is very different for each individual. For one person, it's meditation; for the next, it's playing the piano; for the third martial arts; for the fourth, cooking. However, I would say that most people have no idea what it actually is for them. And you don't find that out by thinking about it or doing psychotherapy but by trying different things and *feeling* how they make you feel. Vitality is, first of all, something physical. The second way to strengthen resources is to do something that definitely leads to more relaxation and vitality for everyone at the same time: sex! And here begins the dilemma.

An alarmingly large number of people suffer from sexual aversion or even sexual dysfunction, ranging from 20 to almost 50 percent, depending on the study. Both men and women are affected. In men, this phenomenon manifests itself primarily in the fact that they can't; in women, it is in the fact that they don't want to.

Are Exhaustion in Life and Exasperation with Sex Related?

Appetite Comes with Eating

The main reason healthy people don't have sex is probably "I'm too tired." Couples who engage in sex experiments à la "Just do it" (Douglas Brown) and have sex every day for a certain time report that it is, above all, discipline that is needed to be able to have sex every day. Of course, you are exhausted in the evening after a super-full day at work, possibly with children and household. But it's not just the exhaustion of a hard and long day at work and falling into bed late that makes us tired of sex. We often just can't get up the nerve, even though we have the time.

Maybe it works the other way around: that exhaustion disappears *when* you pick yourself up and that the lust for life comes back *when* you activate the sex drive. Just like the desire for a delicious meal sometimes comes only when you have the first bite in your mouth. For me, it's very often like that. Well, not while eating, because I'm actually always hungry, but actually during sex. In normal everyday life, I'm often just tired in the evening, and in the morning when I wake up, I don't get going right away either. During the day, I'm always busy with something else. But when my partner tenderly comes around the corner and just starts, I like to join in. I have never experienced sex that was not fun for me, and I have always felt better afterward than before. Enough burnout—bring on the sex!

Sex, in any form, is an excellent source of energy. People who suffer from burnout do not have sex or have it only very rarely. They don't feel any desire, and in the case of men, the decisive part of the body no longer plays along. An acquaintance of mine, a therapist, says quite succinctly that she has never come across a burnout patient in whom sexuality plays any role at all. Are sexual disorders the result of burnout? Or are they possibly also the cause? Could it not be that burnout is becoming more and more common *because* so many people have so little sex? And that sex would be a very effective therapy? Burnout and sexual disorders both frequently occur, especially in modern societies. In the *DTV-Atlas Sexuality*, I read something interesting on this subject, namely that sexual disorders are a product of the respective culture, both in terms of their frequency and their manifestation. In cultures that affirm rather than demonize sex, erectile dysfunction is virtually nonexistent. In sexually repressive cultures, on the other hand, it is commonplace. That would mean, however, that we are by no means as sexually liberated in our culture as we think we are. And that, too, can be explained. According to sociologists, sexual behavior is not "drive-driven" but controlled by so-called social scripts. The thought behind this is that every person comes into the world with complete sexual potential, just as he or she brings the potential to speak. Toddlers can learn any language if they are given an appropriate opportunity, even several at the same time. The languages the children learn and whether they fully exploit the potential depend on their environment, how they are encouraged, and what they enjoy.

Our problem with sex is that we are influenced by many different "scripts" that contradict one another. For example, the Ministry of Health recommends condoms, and the church forbids them. Parents and teachers teach young people that they should not have sex until they are adults, if possible, but their friends all say that they have already had sex. On the one hand, men are supposed to understand women and show emotion, and on the other, they are taught that they have to be strong and masculine. Women are fully emancipated nowadays and know what they want, but at the same time, they learn from their mothers that they should hold back when it comes to men and sex. These contradictory messages create confusion that becomes stronger the more social and cultural scripts influence a person. The result of these contradictions is inner conflict, uncertainty, and, not infrequently, great stress.

What are your deep, inner beliefs about sex? Especially about sex, the way you like it best? What makes you feel guilty just thinking about it? Questioning the scripts that make us tick is a very exciting business because we are usually not aware of them at all, just as we don't think about the fact that we speak our mother tongue. We just do. But we come into conflict when the script doesn't work, when it competes with our fun, or when we suddenly feel we want something but somehow are not allowed to have it. The bad thing is that we learn the sex- and fun-hostile scripts much earlier than the fun-friendly ones; they are much older and make their mischief in our subconscious. We learn certain sentences, rules, and commandments in elementary school. Imagine that you accumulate heaps of such scripts and beliefs in your subconscious during your life and constantly experience inner conflicts that you consciously don't even notice. And this is in such a fundamental area of life as sexuality. No wonder if someone then burns out. But not many have yet come to the idea that this could play a role. Burnout issues are discussed almost exclusively in the context of professional activity, and the culprits are mainly the evil big companies that finish off their employees. And most offers for the treatment of burnout are directed only at the symptoms because the cause lies somewhere else entirely.

Exhaustion has to do with not living out our sexuality and with having too little fun in life! Start to strengthen your resources—have more sex and have more fun! Ask your doctor or alternative practitioner if he or she can prescribe sex for you. Maybe then there will eventually be a health insurance that will pay the costs of toys and lingerie.

"When you are all woman, you are pure energy!"

Interview with Roswitha Sedlmayr, Managing Director of the Sedlmayr Sanatorium in Bad Tölz, Bavaria (https://sanatorium-sedlmayr.de)

Roswitha, for many years you have been treating people in your sanatorium with physical and mental problems. What role does sexuality play there?

A big one. Even a very big one. For people to talk honestly about their sexuality, they need a lot of trust and a safe space. Both with me—on the one hand, I am trustworthy, and on the other hand, I am bound to professional secrecy. Many clients have said to me, "I have been in therapy for many years, but it is only with you that I can open up to this topic."

Do you address this directly?

Frequently, yes. When people come to me with breakup stories, loneliness, depression, burnout, or a borderline diagnosis, then of course I also ask them about their sexuality if they don't start talking about it on their own. Often they have a strong need for it. You can imagine it like this: People come from a gray everyday life, and they themselves are also pale and colorless. They have literally lost their color and expression and are far away from themselves. Maybe I should start taking before and after photos because there are worlds in between.

What does a therapy in your sanatorium look like?

In our house we usually start with the body, with vitalizing it and get it in shape. Nutrition, for example, is a very important topic. First of all, we give the organism the nutrients it needs to become healthy. Through nutrition, exercise, and sport, and of course through the various treatments (massages) to relieve the many hardenings and tensions in the muscles. The point is to make the body permeable again. Only then does the person begin to feel. For example, to feel which needs he actually has. Most people no longer know what really does them good!

What diagnoses do people mainly come with, and how long do they stay?

We have a lot of clients from the psychosomatic field, for example, with the diagnosis of burnout. Nowadays, there is really no clinical picture that does not have a psychovegetative-accompanying diagnosis. In the meantime, this has even become a diagnosis for in-patient treatment, that is a cure, in our country. In the past, people came mainly because of orthopedic and internal medicine diagnoses, but this is becoming less and less common. Today it is mostly a general state of exhaustion, accompanied by physical symptoms. Our patients stay on average three to six weeks.

What happens to people when they talk openly about their sexuality?

First of all, this is a topic that is still very much taboo; people don't talk about it, especially not with their work colleagues. Often even not with their friends. It's something intimate, and still very shame- and guilt-ridden; a lot of things come up in our conversation. I think it's really our upbringing, religion, these many inner rules and moral dogmas that we carry within us, that prevent us from experiencing this wonderful gift in its full dimension.

Where do men "hang" the most?

Most men say, "My wife doesn't feel like it and we haven't had sex for two years," or "We only have sex once a month now." They want more and are totally frustrated because they don't know how to get it. Often, these are very faithful men who don't want to cheat at all because they love their wives and want to maintain the relationship. They are often completely desperate because they are missing something very important. In the course of therapy we work out how a man can deal intensively with his wife and stand up for his wishes and needs. This is very difficult for many men; they don't want to confront their wife because they are afraid of destroying the harmony.

Well, the "harmony" is then probably rather superficial. And what is the main issue with women?

Many women want a sensitive, loving man who gives them time. They want to feel security, need it slowly and not fast sex. Rubbing and speed—most women don't want that. The woman should be the teacher for the man. But not vice versa. She must know that she is the teacher. She sets the tempo, the rhythm, and not the man. These are real qualities of the feeling woman. The man wants something from the woman and the woman wants something from the man.

Shouldn't everyone start with themselves first?

Of course, in my work the focus is on the individual and not on the couple. This means that the man has to rediscover his masculine strength and the woman her feminine. A man learns to be a man, only with another man, and there the relationship with the father plays a big role. This is a dilemma because most men neither know nor can use the power from their paternal lineage. For women, the same is true of the maternal line. The point is discovering oneself, one's own power. For example, I also teach women to do self-love. Touching oneself is very foreign to many; most have never looked at themselves, don't even know what their female genitals look like.

What do people need to dare to live their sexuality?

First and foremost, they need access to their own bodies. That is the foundation. Most people are so far away from themselves, they don't feel themselves anymore; they are cut off. This includes moving, sweating, smelling, perceiving oneself with all with all senses, breathing! Get out of your head, away from your thoughts. The body provides everything I need, but I have to rediscover that first. I can only experience pleasure through the body.

Some people claim that 90 percent of sexuality takes place in the head.

Well, a lot happens in the brain during orgasm. But that's much later. To get into pleasure, I need the body. This is my temple. Libido is something that happens in all cells. In tantra, for example, there are exercises in which you learn to make all the cells in the body vibrate. And you can learn to have an orgasm that spreads throughout the whole body and beyond.

Your own path to fulfilling sexuality also went through tantra?

For a long time I was on the road in the classical way—family, children, career. I ran a family business for over twenty years and lived a full life, but somehow something essential fell by the wayside.... I have always been interested in how to bring sex and heart together. I experimented a lot in the field of sexuality before I got married, but actually I was always looking for love. Later I learned psychotherapy, different kinds of bodywork, all kinds of things. That was highly exciting, but what I always missed was sexuality, which is excluded in most therapies. The individual as a being in his nakedness and in his true nature is not nature; that is not seen at all. Then I came to tantra and suddenly found everything there: sexuality, psychology, and spirituality. It was like a revelation, a feeling of "being whole." I would like to share these experiences with other people!

You live in the down-to-earth Bad Tölz in the deepest Upper Bavaria. How can you share your experiences there?

I decided to focus more on these very normal needs of people in our spa business. For example, how can I create a fulfilling sex life for myself? This is something that everyone wants. As I said, it is often a topic in individual therapy anyway. In addition, I am increasingly offering more lectures for the spa guests and hold courses in breathing meditation, for example. I would also like to offer more seminars in the Munich area so that I can reach even more people.

Sexuality often unfortunately still has something "dirty" in public.

I was just recently on an international tantra seminar in France; there were many very educated and interesting people, therapists, academics of all disciplines. It was not "dirty" at all. Sexuality in itself is in principle of course an issue for all people somewhere. My experience, however, is that people who attend congresses on this topic are simply more curious and more open to further education and development in this area, and to grow as a result. However, many people first want to discover all this for themselves and are often not yet ready to go public with these topics and to show themselves.

Perhaps it would be good and would already be enough if we ourselves begin to think about it differently—we who write and teach about it.

The message is actually simple: you are welcome, with what makes you. Nothing and nobody is worth less or more or deviant or whatever. Everything is allowed to show, to express, to be. This is a great invitation. You are welcome with everything; you are okay the way you are. Just through this healing can happen. Sex is something wonderful, something beautiful, and it is an incredible source of power. In the pelvis is the greatest power available to us. I can learn to feel this power in my body, to direct it and use it, for example, for my steadfastness, intuition, alignment and clarity, for empathy and compassion, for my self-expression, maybe even for my enlightenment. Therefore, sexuality is something sacred for me and nothing dirty!

How can sex lead to enlightenment?

I have already had unbelievable experiences myself—for example, the energy from the pelvis up through my body and reach a state of pure consciousness. This is actually a masculine quality, pure consciousness. The female quality is pure energy. A woman who is completely herself, in her femininity, who is completely in her body, feels energy in every cell. This is fantastic! I wish that many women [could] experience this! We have the possibility to feel and establish both qualities, the animus and the anima, within ourselves so that we can do something with them in real life. When I can live and unite these two aspects in me, I don't need anything more from my partner. I am no longer needy; I don't need to use the other to fulfill my needs. Then a completely different dimension of sexuality is possible.

That sounds very exciting but also very spiritual. What can Erna and Heinz-Uwe do, simple people who read this book and can't or don't want to dive into the depths of sacred sexuality right away?

(Laughs) Just start! The most important thing, in my opinion, is to date. Make a time, once a week, sit down together and share.

Take your time. A real date, without kids, TV or phone. It's about being present, really being there for the other person. That's what makes the other person feel seen. The ticket is eye contact. When that is given, doors open. Then the man can conquer the woman again. It takes this entrance ticket. For the woman in any case, because she does not want to just be screwed once a week. The sexual energy of the woman is in the heart, in the breasts, so we need foreplay, time together. Loving is something you have to learn. It's not something you just get, you don't learn it at school—you have to make an effort yourself!

Thank you for this inspiring conversation!

EPILOGUE

Arrived. Now life is really getting started.

I think sex is a beautiful thing between two people.
Between five—fantastic!

— Woody Allen

Grünwald, August 2012. It's hot. Really hot. Summer at last! I sit on the balcony and enjoy the silence. Many are on vacation, only a dog in the neighborhood barks from time to time, and the wind blows softly through the trees. My belly is getting fatter, six months. It is well known by now that humans learn and get a lot even before birth, and since my life is quite varied, my "roommate" already gets a lot of impulses. Yesterday, the little human in my belly had a whole new experience: trance music and happy hormones. I was with my partner at one of the most awesome fetish parties I have ever attended in my life: SubRosaDictum, "the secret garden." Location: a greenhouse and garden. Atmosphere: incredible. A mild summer night (which is really rather rare in Munich), people in the craziest outfits, pillories, cages, and St. Andrew's crosses next to palm trees and ivy vines, couples who are enraptured in a game and others who watch curiously, in between the one or other place where tenderness is exchanged. Horny! As a pregnant woman, being at such parties again is something very special. I bought myself a new latex dress in which the belly still fits. However, I had to change the silver platform boots soon, and out of consideration for my roommate, I

169

did not stay long in the loud music. He can already hear everything now. Soon I will also play Mozart for him. But this hour of trance dancing between the palm trees had to be. The happiness hormones were bubbling away, and many of my acquaintances there were tenderly stroking my belly. And I realized once again, *this is my thing*. I have arrived. It's enough just to be there, in the middle of it, not being able to get enough of these garishly dressed people who show themselves here in a way that probably no one else sees them. Slave, mistress, demon, pony, slut, drag queen, gladiator. The mind is silent on such evenings; the everyday problems are left with the everyday clothes in the wardrobe. I look forward to everything that is yet to come, and so does my partner. There is still so much to discover. Actually, I have only just begun.

What actually happens when you have experienced Life Changing Sex? That is a good question. Maybe you want to start sharing this fantastic experience with other people. That's why I'm writing this book. How many people stagger through life with nothing but unfulfilled dreams, always thinking in categories of "I would, would have, wish, would actually want someday …" Let's assume you still have one year to live. Would you then dare more, try more, live more intensively? Would you no longer hold back constantly and everywhere because someone expects it of you? There is so much more in life, people—you can't imagine! Becoming free in the area of sexuality is the greatest gift people can give themselves. Exploring what makes you happy also makes you healthy. Mentally healthy. It's not just about sperm being a good source of zinc if you consume it regularly. It's about more, about being alive. People are doing all sorts of things to improve their health, their weight, dieting, and therapy after therapy, not seeing that the simplest solution is right in front of them: Live what's inside you. All of it! Bring your dark side to light and have fun with it!

Surely one or the other thinks now, *Well, great, she makes a good speech. She has no family and can do what she wants. With me, it is completely different; all this does not work!* Or maybe you complain that you don't have a partner and that sex doesn't work for you anyway. People who are not successful, no matter in which area, look for reasons. People who are successful are looking for solutions. I have created my life the way it suits me, and I have chosen a partner who takes me exactly as I am. And that is the way I *really* am. It is not a question of being able but of wanting. And it's a question of curiosity. I just followed my curiosity and fun, and so can you. Sure, there might be consequences. Because yes, if you want to change your sex life, this inevitably also affects your partner and your relationship! And yes, you will scare some people. But then you know this was real Life Changing Sex.

If you are curious now, start researching. Try it out. It's worth it.

ABOUT THE AUTHOR

The energy is sparkling here! Susanne Wendel is considered Germany's most lively sex and health expert. Her speeches, lectures, workshops, and books sparkle with charm, wit, and competence. The sexologist (MA), certified nutritionist, and successful author has been giving lectures and conducting workshops on health and communication topics for well-known companies and at various events since 2001. In 2007 she gave her first workshop on the topic "Let's Talk about Sex" and participated in many training courses in the field of sexuality. Susanne Wendel completed an international four-year leadership and coaching training (Wailea GmbH & Co KG) from 2008 to 2011 and studied applied sexual sciences at Merseburg University from 2017 to 2022.

Susanne founded Health & Fun GmbH with her husband in the summer of 2012, which markets her books and lectures and organizes speeches, lecture events, and seminars throughout German-speaking countries. Susanne and her husband live near Munich and have two kids.

For more information about the author and her offers, go to www.susanne-wendel.com and www.gesundgevoegelt.com and her Youtube-Chanel: https://www.youtube.com/@gesundgevoegelt

Mail contact: office@susanne-wendel.com

For more information about Susannes Mentor, Sonja Becker, go to: www.radarforleaders.com

Printed in the United States
by Baker & Taylor Publisher Services

Printed in the United States
by Baker & Taylor Publisher Services